D0981836

Your Daughters Shall Prophesy

The seven programs that provide the primary data for this book are often referred to by their acronyms. The programs and the acronyms are as follows:

BWIM   Black Women in Ministry

CWR   Center for Women and Religion

R/RA   Research/Resource Associates Program

SQAG   Seminary Quarter at Grailville

TWFM   Training Women for Ministry

WCT   Women Counseling Team

WTC   Women's Theological Coalition

YOUR DAUGHTERS SHALL PROPHESY

Feminist Alternatives in Theological Education

by
The Cornwall Collective

The Pilgrim Press
New York

Library of Congress Cataloging in Publication Data

Cornwall Collective.
  Your daughters shall prophesy.

  Includes bibliographical references and index.
  1. Clergy, Training of. 2. Theology—Study and teaching—United
States. 3. Sexism in theological seminaries—United States. 4. Racism in
theological seminaries—United States. 5. Women seminaries—United
States. I. Title.
BV4030.C67   1980   207'.73   80-14891
ISBN 0-8298-0404-8

The Pilgrim Press, 132 West 31 Street, New York, New York 10001

Contents

Preface

This book fills a need for those who have written it and for those who will read it. It provides much needed encouragement to women—and to men—who are engaged in the difficult work of re-defining, re-designing, and re-doing theology from within a feminist perspective. It is also a work of encouragement for those of us who have labored in the places where the experiences that are recorded here have happened. It says that we have made some advances and engendered some new life in old soil, no matter that it is very rocky soil indeed. Above all, it says to those who read it that there is no single formula for developing new pedagogies, new curricula, or those support bases (like women's centers and coalitions) that have been so important for women in theological education. It is the hope of the Cornwall Collective that the reader will be stimulated by the variety that is here to see the possibilities in each situation and to discover therein the elements which will be the makings of a plan that can respond to these particular needs.

This book is a reflection, in midstream, of action that is still in progress. It is not a collection of success stories, but it does contain in-depth analyses of a few of the many experiences women have had in searching out new ways of working in the context of theological education. It is, however, not intended to be comprehensive in its scope or perspective; its focus is on analyzing the common themes and experiences of seven programs. A full history of each of these programs and of the movement that helped to cross-fertilize and nurture them waits to be written. Another book is required to bring into one story the vision and the work of the many women who have through conferences, consultations, workshops, caucuses, and committees been the *sourcing* for the programs that are the background for this book.

One Sunday morning in Claremont, California, I talked with two women who will play an important part in recording that history—Nelle Morton and Anne Bennett. They worked with the material we are speaking of like two weavers making a tapestry. Anne held the loom taut and wove in the background, reminding us of the forces from the society that had profound impact on the church, pushing it to change—the civil rights movement, the antiwar movement, the creation of the National Organization for Women—the effects these had on the National Council of Churches and the World Council of Churches, causing both bodies to reorganize their structures and restate their priorities. Nelle worked the shuttle, carrying into the tapestry the varied colors of names like Claire Randall and Thelma Stevens, and the roles each had played in a series of conferences that were the forerunners of the Seminary Quarter at Grailville—Claire by using her good offices as program director for Church Women United, and Thelma by her generosity in making available for women a retirement gift she had received. Nelle recalled the important Grailville conferences of 1968 and 1972, jointly sponsored by Church Women United and The Grail. She mused about whether the first conference for women theologians, held at Alverno College, might have been the place where the idea for the Women's Caucus of the American Academy of Religion was conceived. Both women dialogued a bit about the excitement and the pain of being involved early on in teaching new courses and beginning to glimpse the implications for theology of the new research coming from feminist scholars. Nelle described her own conversion to the women's movement and the role of Church Women United, who hired her to design a series of workshops across the country in order to hear what churchwomen were saying. She sketched the patterns of several separate events and then linked them together into a design that showed both their distinctiveness and the interrelationships between academic and church-based developments in women and theology.

This oral tapestry needs to be translated into print. It will greatly enrich us all and will provide both the breadth of scope and the long perspective that are beyond the range and purpose of this book; it will be a companion volume.

This book focuses on some alternatives to theological education which have developed out of that rich history. As such, it provides an opportunity for reflection, learning, and new energy for those who continue to work toward a vision of an inclusive church and a just society.

Peggy Cleveland
Willits, California

Acknowledgments

We wish to express our appreciation to the Lilly Endowment, Incorporated, for the funding that made possible the consultation from which the material in this book is drawn, and to Sister Mary Hennessey (director, Boston Theological Institute, 1974-77) and the Rev. Yvonne Delk (visiting faculty member, Harvard Divinity School, 1976-77), who shared their ideas and advice with us in the initial planning stages of the project.

We also wish to express our appreciation for a grant from the Gregory Book Fund—administered by the American Missionary Association and the Division of Higher Education of the United Church Board for Homeland Ministries—which helped to make possible the publication of this book.

Introduction

The women whose experiences of theological education are reflected in this book come out of contexts shaped by religious and feminist commitments. The effect of the commitments on our lives varies in the ways we understand and relate to our faith and in the ways we have been influenced by feminist ideologies.[1] Yet, we share the common experience of working in situations in which we are continually confronted with the pervasiveness of sexism in our society.

We understand sexism to be a set of attitudes, behaviors, and societal structures that differentiates between women and men on the basis of their sex in

- —access to resources
- —participation in making and enforcing decisions
- —setting criteria for inclusion/exclusion (e.g., what behavior is acceptable, what constitutes "academic competence," what priorities are set in addressing institutional "needs")
- —the power to name reality.[2]

We are writing out of our own experience of attempting to address sexism in the context of theological education. Our purpose is to reflect on that experience, learn from it, and share it, hoping to push ourselves toward new insights in the process of documenting our experience and experiments, and to clarify our perceptions. In addition, we hope to provide feedback to the institutions of which we are a part.

It is our hope that everyone interested in addressing issues raised by the women's movement in the context of institutional change will find this material helpful. Particular attention is given to material we hope will be of assistance to women in seminaries and churches who are concerned about sexist preparation for ministry. Church people—women and men, lay and ordained—whose churches are affected by ministries distorted by sexist theological education may also recognize in these reflections some of the sources of that distortion and may share some of the vision of society which motivates our commitment to change. Women working in other institutions may find the insights gained from these attempts at effecting change in theological education applicable to their situations. Finally, we see this book as source material to encourage seminary students, faculty, administrators, and trustees to move toward a more wholistic and inclusive approach to theological education.

The way in which we wrote this book is important to our understanding of the significance of the material, and is outlined here to demonstrate some of the processes we consider vital in developing a theology and an understanding of ministry appropriate to a pluralistic world. Collective reflection on shared experience is crucial for such a theology. Hence, we began our work by choosing seven programs as our experiential base and involving nineteen women in reflecting together on the insights drawn from those experiences. The programs which formed that base are:

1. Black Women in Ministry—Boston Theological Institute, Boston, MA
2. Center for Women and Religion—Graduate Theological Union, Berkeley, CA

3. Research/Resource Associates Program—Harvard Divinity School, Cambridge, MA
4. Seminary Quarter at Grailville—Loveland, OH
5. Training Women for Ministry—Andover Newton Theological School, Newton Centre, MA
6. Women Counseling Team—Union Theological Seminary, New York, NY
7. Women's Theological Coalition—Boston Theological Institute, Boston, MA

They were chosen because they have certain characteristics in common:

—They are discrete entities related to schools of theology (and/or consortia of theological schools).
—They focus specifically on issues of concern to women in theological education and ministry.
—Responsibilities for the program are carried on by boards or committees constituted outside the regular academic structure.
—Staff is hired through procedures which are different from those regularly employed by the institution.
—There is an attempt to employ models of leadership that differ from the mainline institutional models; that is, to use collective rather than hierarchical models of decision-making.

The programs were chosen by a coordinating committee[3] appointed by the Seminary Quarter at Grailville (SQAG) to plan a consultation on women's programs in theological education.[4] The coordinating committee sought to draw together persons from several programs, to broaden our own perspectives and to provide resources for persons interested in developing strategies for change in other theological institutions. To accomplish this we decided to attempt a collective writing project. Representatives from each program were invited to participate in the consultation, to be held at The Grail Center in Cornwall-on-Hudson, New York, and to write a short working paper addressing seven questions in relation to their program[5]:

1. Briefly describe the program.
   a. What is its history and structure?
   b. Whom does it serve?
   c. What are its sources of funding?
2. What are the assumptions behind the program design?
   a. Why are the different components included?
   b. What issues are being addressed?
3. How is it related to the institution of which it is a part and/or other institutions that are affected by it?
4. What strategies were used for developing and implementing the program?
5. What are the primary questions/most urgent problems of the program?
6. What do you see to be the major themes/issues with which you are struggling?
7. What are your projections for the future? Where do you go from here?

In addition to the seven women who agreed to write working papers, twenty-two resource women were invited to participate in the reflection process. All participants were asked to commit themselves to a collective writing project, which would develop from work groups formed at the consultation. Thus, the "author" of the book is a collective formed by women with similar concerns and commitments, for the purpose of this work. The name, Cornwall Collective, is drawn from the location of the consultation at the Grail's Center in Cornwall.

Prior to our meeting together, the working papers were

circulated among all consultation participants. The coordinating committee identified recurring themes to present to consultation participants as focal points for our conversations. When the total group gathered, these themes, in addition to those identified by other consultation participants, were discussed, and work groups were formed around themes clustered under the following categories: (1) assumptions about education and vocation; (2) power, institutional change, and leadership; and (3) the significance of racism and constituency in program development.

Of the twenty-nine women who had been invited, nineteen agreed to participate and to be involved in the final reflection and writing process. Of these, four were black; fifteen, white; four were Roman Catholic; fifteen, Protestant. The ages of the women ranged from twenty-five to sixty-five. Theological consortia, in Atlanta, Berkeley, Boston, and Chicago, were represented in addition to seminaries in New York, New Haven, Princeton, and Dayton. The list of participants that follows is divided according to the group with which each worked. Institutional and program names are used for identification purposes:

Group I   Assumptions about education and vocation
           Clarissa Atkinson, PhD; faculty, Boston
               University School of Theology; former
               research/resource associate
           Peggy Cleveland, former codirector, Center
               for Women and Religion
           Sally Dries, director, Ecumenical Women's
               Center, Chicago
           Joan Forsberg, dean of students, Yale
               Divinity School
           Cheryl Giles, alumna, Harvard Divinity
               School; chaplain, Boston College
           Kathy Nickerson, Seminary Quarter at

Grailville; alumna, United Theological Seminary, Dayton

Lynn Rhodes, associate director, field education, Boston University School of Theology; former research/resource associate

Edith Thomas, registrar and director of admissions, Interdenominational Theological Center, Atlanta

Barbara Brown Zikmund, PhD; faculty, Chicago Theological Seminary

Group II   Power, institutional change, and leadership

Janet Kalven, Seminary Quarter at Grailville

Joan Martin, coordinator, Justice for Women program of the National Council of Churches; Seminary Quarter at Grailville; alumna, Princeton Theological Seminary

Deborah Streeter, alumna, Pacific School of Religion

Barbara Waugh, codirector, Center for Women and Religion

Barbara G. Wheeler, president-elect, Auburn Theological Seminary; former director, Women's Theological Coalition

Group III   The significance of racism and constituency in program development

Julianne M. Bousquet, M.Div. candidate, Weston School of Theology

Brinton Lykes, PhD candidate, Boston College; former coordinator of Women's Programs, Harvard Divinity School; Seminary Quarter at Grailville

Susan Moyes, Women Counseling Team;

M.Div. candidate, Union Theological Seminary

Nancy Richardson, director, Student and
Community Life, Boston University
School of Theology; Seminary Quarter at
Grailville; Training Women for Ministry

Adele Smith-Penniman, former director,
Black Women in Ministry; alumna, Harvard Divinity School

The themes addressed by these groups led to the
development of the six chapters which follow. Material was
collected by the coordinating committee, which took
responsibility for the details of editing and preparing the
manuscript for publication. While everyone agreed to the
process of collective reflection and writing, it is important to
note that since the final draft consists of chapters that grew
out of the work of small groups, each chapter represents
the opinions and conclusions of the members of those
groups and other authors designated below. In organizing
the material the committee attempted to be consistent with
the reflective model used throughout the process: examining our assumptions, identifying issues that are central to
who we are, developing alternatives, and moving toward
change.

Since our assumptions about theological education
inform our evaluation of our experience, we begin in
chapter 1 with an examination of those assumptions. Based
on the work of persons in Group I, the writing for the
chapter was done by Clarissa Atkinson, Janet Kalven, Lynn
Rhodes, and Nancy Richardson. As newcomers to the
seminaries, women are acutely conscious of the importance
of who shapes the dialogue and determines the criteria for
"who" and "what" is included as a valid part of the
educational experience. Hence, chapter 2 focuses on
constituencies—whose voices need to be heard? How will

they influence the questions we raise? Because racism is a central problem in the society and in theological education, chapter 3 focuses on the particular dimensions of the problem with which women's programs in theological education must deal. Chapters 2 and 3 grew out of the work of Group III. Writers for chapter 2 were Julianne M. Bousquet, Brinton Lykes, and Adele Smith-Penniman; for chapter 3, Nancy Richardson. Chapters 4 and 5 examine alternative structures and models of leadership, as well as change strategies attempted by women's programs. Group II developed the ideas out of which these chapters were written. The writing was done by Janet Kalven, Deborah Streeter, Barbara Waugh, and Barbara G. Wheeler. Chapter 6 consists of a summary of learnings and recommendations drawn from the reflective process and was written by Brinton Lykes and Joan Martin. The introduction is based on the work of the coordinating committee. After the material was edited and the manuscript prepared by the coordinating committee, the manuscript was submitted to Elaine Huber (former research/resource associate; PhD candidate, Graduate Theological Union) for further editing.

Our work together has confirmed our commitment to the collective process. However, the process did present some difficulties: for writers—representing with accuracy the experiences, insights, and recommendations that were articulated in their groups; for group members—maintaining workable procedures for responding to written drafts in the face of the limitations of time and geography; for the coordinating committee—collecting material and editing it to minimize redundancy and maintain the integrity of group and individual work. It is also important to note that the perceptions, insights, and shape of the materials are limited by who we are: mostly white, mostly Protestant, mostly middle class, mostly representing schools of theology located in or near consortia. We do not claim to speak for all women in theological education, nor to represent all efforts at addressing the problem of sexism as it affects theological education. We do claim to speak authentically out of our experiences and to represent a theological and political perspective that schools of theology must take seriously if issues of justice and liberation are to be addressed.

Nancy Richardson, Project Coordinator
The Cornwall Collective

CHAPTER 1

Toward a Feminist Understanding of Theological Education

From storefront churches to the Vatican, feminists are challenging the institutions of patriarchal religion. We recognize that the church has played (and plays) an enormous role in the creation and maintenance of a sexist society—not only in the obvious sexism of worship and of Sunday school, but in the structures and processes of theological education. The preparation of professional ministers, Protestant as well as Roman Catholic, takes place within institutions that perpetuate injustice and oppression.

It would be wrong to imply that accredited schools of theology are the only vehicles for ministerial education, or that ministry itself can be confined to the traditional roles and functions of "professional" and ordained clergy. A comprehensive study of theological education would include an examination of Bible schools, of "training" schools for missionaries and other lay professionals, and of church school programs that engage laypeople in local parishes in preparation for many forms of ministry. This book focuses on just one dimension of the broad spectrum of theological education: accredited schools of theology, schools attached to universities as well as "free standing" seminaries, both church-affiliated and independent. Those of us who participated in the Cornwall consultation have

1

experienced theological education in its elite form, and our comments reflect that perspective even while they criticize it.

Theological Education Today

Women seminarians in the United States today enter a system of theological education that has its roots in the early nineteenth century. Within a few years of the founding of Andover Theological Seminary (Congregational), in 1809, the Andover curriculum became the model for theological education: it remained the model until the early twentieth century and is influential even today. That first curriculum included courses in Sacred Literature, Christian Theology, Sacred Rhetoric, and Ecclesiastical History.[1] Early in this century there was a significant modification of the curriculum, with the introduction of "practical" courses in religious education, psychology and sociology of religion, liturgics, and preaching.[2] Contemporary curricula conventionally offer "practical" courses, along with three "academic" areas—scripture, church history, and theology. The division between practical and academic disciplines remains in force, although there has been some renaming and revaluation; for example, psychology and sociology of religion, and social ethics may be regarded as academic and offered under the rubric of "Church and Society." Ancient assumptions about what constitutes the "core" curriculum have been canonized.

Organized around disciplines, each with its specialized language and methodology, seminaries have adopted the university model of education, claiming "objectivity" as the rationale for a supposedly value-free approach to scholarship. In fact, of course, scholarship is never value-free, and in the schools under discussion it reflects the attitudes and stance of white, middle-class men. Furthermore, the university model itself, derived from nineteenth-century

2

Tübingen (and before that from thirteenth-century Paris) is hierarchical, competitive, and heavily weighted with class, race, and gender bias. Each professor, working alone and usually in competition with his (sic) colleagues, imparts to students those bits and pieces of a discipline that he and the school (in the modified Andover curriculum) feel the student should learn. When the student has collected enough pieces, she/he graduates and, in the case of doctoral students, proceeds to pass on the slightly used pieces in another classroom. Despite a few attempts at integration—mostly in the form of doctoral exams in which the burden of integration is on the student—the pieces are seldom gathered into a pattern meaningful to the student.

In the present system of promotion and tenure, young scholars are trapped into the self-perpetuating disciplines of the traditional curriculum. Publication is emphasized over teaching as the criterion for reward. Students in turn learn to do research that fits the specialized, departmentalized models of "scholarly" work, and those who attempt to do research that integrates the theory and practice of ministry must rely on their own resources. Too often they are told that their interests are peripheral to the essential tasks of theological education. Consistent with this approach to research, the teaching/learning models typically adhere to what Paulo Freire calls a "banking" concept of education[3]: the professor holds a certain body of knowledge, which he deposits in the brain of the student; the student holds it there until the professor calls for it, when it is returned—perhaps with a little interest, perhaps without, for the student's own ideas are add-ons. In this model, required courses ensure that the student acquires what the white, male, middle-class decision-makers of the school regard as basic preparation for ministry. There is little provision for assisting the student to define learning goals, and little recognition of the resources students bring to the educational process. In such a setting, the perspectives of

3

racial minorities,[4] of the poor, and of women are seen as marginal or are totally excluded.

A Feminist Critique of the Current System

As feminists, we have become increasingly aware of the ways in which women are outsiders to the process of theological education. We are not only physically outside, excluded from positions of power such as faculty appointments and top administrative positions; we are psychically outside, because our history and experience are not taken seriously. Women generally are confined to minor, supportive roles, usually low-level administrative or junior faculty positions, serving at the pleasure of white males who do not hesitate to replace women who "cause trouble." This system reflects and perpetuates the sexism that prevails throughout the life of the church. Theological schools acknowledge, record, and interpret the experience of a minority of people in the Christian tradition, claiming that experience as valid for everyone. We do not reject the entire tradition of theological education, but we do insist that it presents only one perspective on a complex reality. Like every other field, theology has become "professional"; it has its own requirements for acquiring credentials and certification. As people invest time, money, and energy in this process, their livelihood and self-esteem come to depend upon maintaining control of a "certain territory on the knowledge map." Powerful territorial imperatives emerge, and methods are soon developed to discredit those outside. When women challenge the basic assumptions in which these imperatives are rooted, they enter the arena of power politics.

The white male perspective is assumed in theological education to define the totality of Judeo-Christian understandings about God. That perspective is universalized as the norm against which all other "talk about God" is

4

evaluated. Such other talk has been called interesting, relevant, even "liberating" by some liberals, but it is not acknowledged as "theology." Questions raised by women, blacks, Hispanics, Native Americans, and the poor are seen as peripheral. New courses may be invented and added to the core curriculum to deal with the interests of current students, but such courses do not alter the structures or assumptions of the disciplines. There are courses in "New Testament" and in "Women in the New Testament," in "Church History" and in "Women in Church History," but basic educational questions are not addressed.

In introductory courses the works of feminist or liberation theologians still appear at the end of the syllabus as optional choices for papers. However, the perceptions of these theologians have not modified the study or the interpretation of Paul or Aquinas, nor are they regarded as integral to the intellectual and spiritual formation of the minister. The Research/Resource Associates Program (R/RA) at Harvard Divinity School provides excellent examples of this phenomenon. The program was designed to bring women from across the country to do research and to provide Harvard with resources to be used in implementing changes in the core curriculum. Although there have been many positive effects of the program, including courses designed and taught by associates that have served women well, the purpose for which the program was designed has *not* been fulfilled. Not one course designed by an associate has been incorporated into the core curriculum, nor is there any evidence that research done by associates has found its way into the main body of course work offered by other faculty in the various disciplines.[5]

Refusing to acquiesce quietly in the system of traditional theological education, feminists have begun to bring to collective consciousness the history, creativity, insights, and experiences of women in faith communities. Believing that the barriers between disciplines are for the most part arbitrary, that clinical pastoral education is not usefully separated from theology and ethics, that church history is neither teachable nor meaningful without social and economic analysis, and that most of the dissertations stacked in theological libraries were written by, for, and about an elite, feminists have articulated a new set of assumptions, which grow out of women's experience of reality.

Feminist Educational Assumptions

Basic to a feminist approach to theological education is the understanding of education as a wholistic process. The word wholistic is in danger of becoming a cliché, but it is still a convenient shorthand for many of the values feminists want to embody. As we attempt to give specific content to the word, its meaning is clarified. Wholistic learning involves both cognitive and affective aspects, and can be expressed in part by such phrases as "knowledge is total experience," or "knowing embraces theory and practice." Dualisms of thought and feeling, being and doing, contemplating and acting, personal and public, sacred and profane create their own demons. Rather than define these aspects of reality as though each had a life of its own, feminists struggle to discover the web of interconnectedness that leads to the formation of images of wholeness. Without such images, fruitless discussions about the relative merits of one side or the other of a dichotomy (for example, the primacy of the academic over the practical fields of theological education) continue to blunt the energy and creativity of both women and men. A call to wholeness affirms that human beings learn through multiple avenues—through the senses, feelings, intuitions—and that learnings can be expressed in many ways—through image and symbol, poetry, dance, and story, as well as through analytical prose. The collection of prose, poetry, and

6

drawings called "The Lady Who Used to Be a Strawberry"[6] is just one example of the work accomplished in courses based on a wholistic approach to theological education. The collection was developed by participants in a course offered through the Graduate Theological Union by the Center for Women and Religion (at that time, 1974, called the Office of Women's Affairs). The course, entitled "Women/Yoga/Creativity," combined the reading and discussion of works by feminist writers, the body movement and reflective discipline of yoga, and the creative expression of participants.[7]

In the context of a wholistic approach, theological education can most effectively attend to its primary task: the preparation of women and men for ministry. In such a context, intellectual understanding is integrated with the development of skills. Instead of the hierarchical, fragmented, departmentalized, competitive approach derived from university models, wholistic approaches are learner-centered, experience-based, open-access and cooperatively oriented. When students learn only in a setting in which one man (usually the case) is "in charge" and has all the knowledge to be given out as he chooses to those over whom he holds power, they are learning a style of ministry. This style is replicated in the ministry when the one person "in charge" transmits to the church the values represented by hierarchy, fragmentation, and competition. Basic to a feminist understanding of ministry, however, is the assumption that it requires a setting of mutuality in which persons are enabled to value and to name their own experiences, learn from them, and move toward new understandings in the light of their own authority and of cooperative power relations.

Mobilized by our critique of the present system of theological education, and energized by our vision of the possibilities of alternative approaches, women around the country have attempted to develop programs based on

7

feminist assumptions and through them to affect the larger system of theological education.

Educational Implications of Feminist Assumptions

In discussions of the curriculum appropriate to a feminist vision of theological education, four overlapping questions recur. First, what teaching and learning forms permit and foster wholistic, experience-oriented education? Second, what should the content of such education be: must the traditional curriculum be replaced (and if so, with what?), or can it be modified to serve our goals? Third, what would "research" mean in a seminary informed by a feminist perspective? Fourth, how would such an institution be organized?

A primary goal of all our programs has been the sharing of knowledge and ideas. Sharing has reinforced the conviction that collaborative, problem-centered, and experience-based forms of learning and teaching are most effective. The associates in R/RA at Harvard are attached to separate departments, but a persistent and successful aspect of the program has been the associates' collaboration with and learning from one another. Through their interaction they have discovered resources for their own work and an affirmation of the educational assumption that interconnections really do exist. We have found that conferences organized around cross-disciplinary topics have been helpful—notably the conference on Black Women and the Black Religious Experience, sponsored by Black Women in Ministry (BWIM) and Harvard Divinity School's Office of Women's Programs in the spring of 1977. Black women ministers and black church women gathered to discuss their own questions, which were not defined by departments, and found the meeting inspirational, informative, and strategically helpful.

8

The Seminary Quarter probably represents the most consistent application of the principles of experiential and self-directed learning. At Grailville the questions of the participants are the questions of the curriculum: "peers are seen as resources, and resource persons as co-learners." Education that does not divide its affective and cognitive aspects is desirable for everyone and may be especially so for women, whose self-confidence frequently has been limited by their life circumstances. If we act on our understanding that the personal is political and the political, personal, the creative energy of the individual flows into the classroom, and the class returns its collective wisdom to the individual.

It is precisely this reality that makes feminist critiques so threatening to traditional models of education. When we raise questions of experiential learning, we inevitably raise questions of personal integrity and truth-telling. Academic excellence is more easily defined in narrow scholastic terms than by asking questions such as "What is the power distribution in the classroom?" and "How do people's experiences affect what/how we learn?" As we raise questions in this larger context, we are no longer dealing with a remote, impersonal discipline but are in fact calling upon one another to relate theory to practice in the learning process itself. This means that the ethical integrity of faculty *and* student is integrally related to the subject matter: we are not grappling only with whether someone has "knowledge of the discipline," but with how that "knowledge" affects their lives. Questions then arise as to how an Old Testament professor, for example, can teach a course in Jeremiah and refuse to take a stand on current social issues. The standards to which a professor of Christian social ethics is held are not just academic; they involve ethical decisions both in the classroom and in the public world. The power of the teacher in the classroom is not just a question of how people learn best, but has ethical dimensions; public issues and how faculty and students relate to them are matters for collective reflection and *mutual* critique. In such a process, personal questions are recognized and valued as theological, ethical, historical, and psychological; cooperative styles of ministry are developed; and the authority derived from mutuality is recognized as real.

In our programs we associate education with consciousness-raising in its best sense, because we believe that education has always been and is necessarily a most important form of socialization and politicization. In consciousness-raising we bring to awareness a critical perspective on the factors that shape and affect our lives. Then we are empowered to make decisions and choose options out of a more comprehensive view of who we are in the midst of our world. The hidden assumptions of "objective" scholarship are much more dangerous than a political awareness that states its goals and proceeds to examine material in the light of avowed belief. We have discovered, to no one's surprise, that the presence of a number of women in a program or a faculty allows each to emphasize her individual understanding of the relationship of content and consciousness. No woman can represent Woman, and tokenism makes nonsense of our goals. The collaborative creativity that has emerged at the Center for Women and Religion (CWR) of the Graduate Theological Union or from the BWIM program is made possible by the coming together of many women who share their separate experience in the light of common political, social, and religious goals.

Today, when many women students in seminaries accept the rewards but do not recollect the struggles for present gains, the companionship and support of other feminists is critical to our attempts to reform theological education. Of our several collaborative efforts—both collaborative learning styles and collaborative strategies for change—the most

10

useful exemplum may be the Training Women for Ministry (TWFM) program, which develops collective modes of ministry and exposes students to a "variety of models . . . which encourage each [student] in developing her own unique understanding and form of ministry." This is not easy, for continual planning and evaluation are as costly in time, money, and energy as they are essential. The model as well as the achievements of TWFM are extremely valuable, but the problems of limited resources have not been solved.[8] The model demands time. It develops strong internal motivation for learning but does not easily achieve systematic and in-depth exploration of issues. This model of learning involves risk, because it asks for self-direction as well as collective responsibility.

If seminary curricula were interdisciplinary, experiential, self-directed, consciousness-raising, and collaborative—in other words, in the *eschaton*—what would happen to its "subjects"? Will our curriculum be radically new, or will we pour the old subjects into new wineskins? Probably that question cannot be answered, or even addressed effectively, until more changes have been made, perhaps because we, too, have been trained in the old schools. In our various attempts to modify both wine and wineskins we have learned that teaching our own course around the edges of the sacred disciplines makes little or no change in what is still perceived as the "mainstream." The only exception to this seems to be in the "practical fields" (e.g., TWFM), which are themselves more often than not considered to be outside the mainstream in the traditional three-disciplines-plus-practical model.

One way to confront stubborn resistance to change is to ask new questions of old material. Read Luther, but ask questions about the shift from a monastic to a familial ecclesiology and its implications in people's lives. Find out about popular religion, not only as it relates to mainstream theology, but in the experience of those who never heard of

11

thirteenth- or twentieth-century scholasticism. CWR defines its work in part as "to describe the human more fully," and that needs to be done in every department of theological education—history, scripture, ethics, psychology. Simply to look with new perceptions at the traditional material can be a catalyst for radical change.

The critical task alone is enormous. CWR speaks of looking at "the fundamental patriarchal mentality that pervades Judeo-Christian theology and the cultures, values, mores, and institutions that have developed from that matrix." Many of us are engaged in such criticism and in the creation that arises from the critical, but we are also involved in the development of material that has not hitherto been recognized or studied in schools of theology. This new material can be described in part as the insight and experience of the dispossessed, of those who are not and have not been the Western white male professors/thinkers/priests/administrators. By its very existence, BWIM creates new material. Their experience, and the experience of all women in theological education, *is* an important part of the new material of seminary curricula. These experiences do give us clues for new curriculum. We need to be intentional, not only about content, but about the diversity of participants, the place in which the curriculum is developed, and in field and experiential components.

Our methodology for the establishment and description of new curricula has been substantially exemplified in TWFM, perhaps because of its relative autonomy and its tradition of leadership by women ministers. The leaders are what they teach, embodying a relation of theory and practice, action and reflection, that is intrinsic to our methodology. We do not accept the old idea that one person—"the scholar"—reads the Greek New Testament, while another—"the minister"—preaches the gospel, and a third—"the reformer"—tries to bring in the kingdom.

12

Scholarship, ministry, and reform are the three bases of our vocational, intellectual, and professional goals.

"Research," the word and the activity, is widely misunderstood in our culture and most seriously misused in the pursuit of the esoteric and the "objective." No research is objective; in capitalist society, research is a commodity supported and directed by those who pay for it. When, for example, researchers study "poor people" or "Latin American women," the work is unlikely to be of value or interest to the people studied. We believe that research can be done collectively, that it is most valuable when it arises out of real questions (not academic "questions"), that researchers should state their biases and communicate in ordinary, nonelitist language available to interested people. We do not conceive research to be an operation that excludes, but an avenue of empowerment to more people in more places, and we reject the old notion of the scholar who "knows more and more about less and less until he (sic) knows everything about nothing." The result of the inclusion of feminist consciousness into research content and methodology will be to change perceptions of reality, presenting new options and new challenges to what has been perceived as foundational.

The changes advocated here in teaching and learning forms, curriculum content, and research require that seminaries do more than add feminist books to their reading lists and a few women to their faculties. They will require major changes in the structure of the institutions themselves, a redistribution of power, and open decision-making procedures. As we have attempted to challenge the structures and content of theological education, we have often found ourselves involved in a tangle of theological discourse, politicking, power plays, and strategies to gain financial resources. We have addressed the essential questions and have argued convincingly that our concerns are central to the issue at hand, only to find ourselves

13

defeated by a technicality (i.e., the committee of which we are part is "only advisory"; the dean makes budget allocations, and in light of a budget deficit . . .). The energy and creativity needed to forge new forms and new programs are often dissipated in the struggle simply to enter the arena where the decisions are made. So long as decision-making procedures in schools of theology are hidden and are controlled by white middle-class males, preparation for ministry occurs in a place that is itself oppressive and therefore negates the gospel call for liberation. A feminist theology of education insists that faith requires an understanding of economic and political reality in order for ministry to be engaged in an ongoing process of liberation. It is crucial, therefore, that institutions of theological education develop structures which encourage a more inclusive pattern of staffing, a more diverse student body, and an environment that reflects the social, political, and economic needs of our time.

Perhaps it is here, as we engage the issues of power politics, that our past feelings of rage or helplessness, of being treated like pawns by powerful institutions (church/university/seminary) may have served us well. They have forced us to recognize the need for collective strategies and have put us in touch with other "outsiders" who have dared to speak out of their own perspectives, to share their own experiences, and to press for change in the basic assumptions about and in the structure of theological education.

CHAPTER 2

Constituency: What We Learn Is Shaped by Those with Whom We Learn

Feminists involved in theological education in the 1960s and 1970s have participated in the women's movement in a special way. We have known that struggle for liberation out of the particular experiences of white male dominated seminaries and schools of theology. We have explored the misogynist roots of patriarchal religion and have begun to name a religious experience "beyond God the Father." The subgroup of our consultation that examined the issue of constituency consisted of five women: one is black, four are white; some are working class, some are middle class; some are Catholic, some are Protestant; some are lesbian, some are heterosexual or bisexual; all have physical traits which distinguish us from one another; all belong to that particular group of women in this country who are being or have been theologically educated. Members of the group have worked with most of the programs represented at the consultation; that is, with Seminary Quarter at Grailville (SQAG), Black Women in Ministry (BWIM), the Women Counseling Team (WCT), the Research/Resource Associates Program (R/RA), and Training Women for Ministry (TWFM).

The word constituency may seem strange in a context that has clearly defined its constituency as women. But we discovered early in our work within the women's movement that women are not a unitary group. We talk about ourselves and others in terms of sex, race, class, religion, age, sexual preference and physical characteristics. These descriptors are used to differentiate us from one another or to group us with others. Although the combinations of these various descriptors that highlight the diversity among humans are multiple, they also form an interdependent matrix which describes our inner and social selves. I can tell you who I am by describing one or another dimension of myself; that is, I am female, or I am twenty-nine years old. I tell you more about myself if I say that I am a twenty-nine-year-old white, upper-middle-class Catholic. I could tell you still more by adding my family size, the area of the country in which I was raised, or my sexual preference. In this way I locate myself in a social network, as well as describe some aspects of my self-identity.

These identifying words are used for self-definition. They name our relationships to other individual persons or to groupings. They have also been used by the self to name the "other" and to name the social environment. And it is in this process of self-definition and in definition of/or by the other that conflict often emerges in relation to the question of constituency. Who is defined as similar, and who is defined as different, and why? What are the criteria for such definitions? Are they implicit or explicit? By whom are they determined?

As women in theological education, we experience the dominant culture of white males to be the primary "namer." We experience ourselves as the named and then are required to act in ways that legitimate the ways in which we have been named. Our struggle has been, in part, one of trying to shift the burden of proof to those who are doing the naming. We have been excluded from access to resources, from power, and from decision-making. We refuse to continue to be expected to justify *why* we want the distribution of power to be equalized.

16

But our situation is much more complex. All of us belong, in some way, to that group which is in power. At the very least, all of us have risen in class and status to that elite group which is theologically educated. Hence we move between the established sources of power and our own particular experiences of being excluded from this power. We have found some solidarity with one another as women. But even there we encounter dissonance due to religious or sexual preference, race, or class; we know that exclusion exists in significant ways within our own sex. Our experience, then, is a complex web of being in and being out—and of searching for an "I," a "we" in the midst of ever changing social reality which is, paradoxically, rigidified in seemingly unchanging social structures.

As we have begun to experience personal power as women through consciousness-raising groups, classroom experiences, or on the street, we have begun to name our experiences and to rename ourselves. We refuse to be defined primarily or exclusively in terms of our relationship to men: wife, mother, student, lover. We reject religious models that image us as pure Virgin or as seductive Eve. We speak of our strength as persons and as women. We are, as Nelle Morton has described it, sharing an "aha" experience and "hearing one another into speech." In daring to name ourselves we have also begun to dare to name the "problem" as outside ourselves. We have begun to question the very nature of that which has always been named "reality." We see that it was a particular experience of reality—known to white males in power—and that that particular reality has made claims to being universal.

As we started to see that our choices were to maintain our secondary status or to struggle for full personhood, we opted for the struggle. Some questioned this strategy from the start. Others needed some experiences of defeat or of victory before beginning to raise more fundamental

17

questions about the rules of the game. Our vision of social reality, based on our experiences, was valid. It was not exclusively hierarchical. It did not depend on "power over" but on empowerment. We formed groups and began the process of support and self-criticism, criticism of ourselves and of the systems we were shaping and being shaped by. We began to develop concrete strategies for social change.

This process of naming was and is shaped by the constituencies represented therein; and it shapes these and other constituencies. It is not a neutral process. In its roots it is class-based, based on the reflections of women with access to the leisure time needed for advanced theological education. This insight does not minimize the power and empowerment of the experiences we have known and out of which we have come to name our "liberating idea." But it does indicate that we too are shaped by the matrix we seek to reshape, and that who we are as a group influences the naming process, the vision we articulate, and the strategies we develop.

Hence it is critically important to acknowledge the parameters of our constituency, and to recognize the extent to which the original namers and sharers of an experience shape its future direction. What follows in this chapter is, then, a clarification of certain aspects of the question of constituency.

The working group on constituencies chose to explore three of the many dimensions that describe one's under-standing of self and others—race, class, and sexuality. These three dimensions have been primary sources of naming our constituencies as women in theological education. They have also been most salient in our struggles. We examined the dynamics of being included or excluded because of race, class, or sexuality, struggling to understand the relationship of inclusion or exclusion in shaping our programs. As a result, we have provided some working definitions and have articulated the ways in which we have experienced race, class, and sexuality in our work within theological education. (Because race has been a central shaping force in our lives and in much of our work, we have chosen to discuss it more fully in the next chapter, particularly as it has been experienced and expressed in our programs.) We have also become increasingly sensitized to other defining characteristics, such as age differences and Christian versus post-Christian feminist perspectives.

Concern with constituency has been a dynamic part of our ongoing development. It can serve as a prophetic force, pushing us to name the ways in which the present system oppresses all who are not white, male, heterosexual, and healthy. Or it can slow us down, diverting our attention into seeking the least common denominator in all that we do so that we do not exclude anyone. Here we examine our experiences at both extremes of this dichotomy, and in successful and unsuccessful efforts at compromises, and lift up the ways in which constituency issues have shaped and been shaped by our struggles within theological education.

Race

In sharing our personal journeys and work lives we were immediately struck by differences due to race, and how such differences and our awareness of them and commitments to struggle with them shaped the programs we coordinated and participated in. We named the differences and formulated a definition of how we saw racism functioning at the personal and the systemic levels in our society (see chapter 3). We then sought to explore our work within the theological context in an effort to understand more fully the ways in which we had succeeded and failed in addressing these concerns.

The SQAG and R/RA provide two parallel examples. Both programs were designed by white women who felt they had struggled with racism, in their own lives and in society, and who had a commitment to create programs that addressed the concerns and educational needs of all women, not only of white middle-class women. Further, the designers had sought to create an educational context that would provide tools for analyzing racism and the ways in which it functions in society and, in particular, within religious institutions. From the outset the participation of racial minority women was sought in the programming at all organizational levels. The paternalism inherent in attempting to involve black women in programs designed by white women was not recognized. Black women had not been sought out in their context in an effort to understand their questions and support their struggle. White women had assumed the importance of their struggle and wanted it to be reshaped in light of the involvement of black women, but they were not conscious of the extent to which it would have been defined differently if a collaborative, peer relationship with black women had been engaged at the outset. A closer look at the SQAG program will clarify this process of self-discovery of the depths of our racism and, more specifically, how it permeates the very structure of our language.

In 1976 SQAG had its largest participation of racial minority women. The significance of this level of diversity, as manifested in a shift in the *context* of learning, had immediate implications for the *content* of the learning process. One illustration of this centered around a discussion of differing understandings of power. White women were struggling to learn to use the word power to describe themselves, affirming the importance of the psychological growth witnessed to by them and their sisters. Black women, whose understanding of power was shaped by the Black Power movement, were somewhat skeptical of such usage, having experienced the male dominance of that movement, as well as the frustration of recognizing that the movement never really achieved the kind of political and economic power necessary for substantive change. Latin American women brought another perspective to the discussion, sharing the Spanish word for power *(poder)* and its meaning related to socioeconomic control. They differentiated it from *dynamos*, which means personal energy, and insisted that *poder* was neither a word that reflected women's position nor one they would use to describe their goals. This discussion led to a deeper knowledge of the cultural and class biases of language and to new understandings of the complexity of experiences.

Hence it was discovered that the racial composition of SQAG 1976 participants, staff, and resource persons shaped the educational experience of all involved in a new way. White women were able to explore intellectually, spiritually, and emotionally the roots of their prejudice and to test these against concrete experiences of others, which showed them that what they had grown to see as normative of women's experience was only normative of white women's experience. For the racial minority women it was one of the few—and for some the only—times that they had not been alone in their theological education, singled out as *the* token. Stated more positively, it was an opportunity for them to come together—in some small way—across their ethnic diversity; for some it was their first experience of women's community.

But the constituency question as it related to race was not resolved by this experience in SQAG 1976. It became clear that a number of factors served to exclude, albeit unintentionally, on the basis of race: the setting in a women's community, the reputation (not entirely accurate) of the program as a post-Christian community, and the location on a farm in Ohio. For racial minority women who recognize the importance of the family in the survival of their communities, who experience the church as a central link to these communities, or who expect to live and work in urban settings, SQAG was exclusive and did not address their reality. Further, for at least one black woman who participated in SQAG, it was an incredibly painful experience—one of being called upon to be the "black mamma" or the "black prophet," of raising white women's consciousness and of "giving them" the liberating idea; "a crucifixion of sorts" were the words she used to describe it. This is a woman who is a leader in her community, a strong, experienced minister and teacher.

Clearly, the program was *not* reflective of the human or educational needs of racial minority women. Thus, the work of women determined to create an alternative, a place where racial minority women and white women could come together to learn of their differences and to begin to articulate a struggle against their common oppression out of those differences, had not succeeded. Yet participants, through ongoing evaluations of the program, honest discussions with one another, and especially through friendships that developed across race and class lines, were enabled to confront these contradictions.

Space does not permit the recounting of SQAG's journey from this point forward. The process of developing new forms goes on. One of the strengths of SQAG lies in the fact that it has continued to struggle with that process and has not opted for easy solutions to very difficult questions.

Discussion in our working group was often painful. Black women who had been hurt by these programs shared their experiences with some of us. White women who had fought so hard to acknowledge their role as white women as both oppressors and oppressed, who had seen themselves as acting in support of their black sisters, began to understand at a deeper level the complexity of the process. And some were able to feel good about the struggles to confront the personal and systemic racism within their lives, within theological education, within women's programs, within the church, and within society.

Class

In discussing the role of class in our working group we struggled to define it as distinct from status and privilege, and to clarify its meaning further in the context of theological education. Group members explored their own class backgrounds in order to describe and understand the ways in which they have shaped their present understandings and beliefs.

One member described childhood in a white working-class community and the extent to which education had been seen as a way to move upward on the class ladder.

> I had always been aware of the ladder and of the fact that everyone didn't make it to the top, or even halfway, but I was told that I was bright and I could do it. And in many ways I am fulfilling that prophecy—I have made it to graduate school, I have moved up. But the costs have been enormous. I find myself in a context—the theological school—which assumes that everyone is middle class, assumptions inherent in its economic policies, its tuition, its style of worship, and its language. And those of us who are not are expected to conform to this system. In many ways that is my expectation of myself—and I can pass. I've learned the language, I've even internalized their way of thinking. But this is not my people and I want to return to my people to minister.

The so-called class mobility has resulted in a crisis of identity, a crisis rooted in class contradiction.

A middle-class black member of the group described her experience as a black in the white communities where she grew up and presently lives.

> I live in a minority position within both communities, yet I am a member of an elite group. I am one of the few black clergy women who has completed a theological degree. I am one of the few blacks who have achieved some form of economic

23

stability. I am one of the few blacks in a white denomination, and I am a woman. I am confronted by these realities in my work with Black Women in Ministry, for there we have struggled to include all black women—clergy, lay, evangelical; those who criticize Christianity; the poor, wealthy, formally educated, and life-tutored. I must own the particularity of my own situation and move out from there to embrace these differences. To be mystified by my own class privilege, or apologetic or guilty for it only leads to confusion, diffusion of goals, and an inability to dialogue.

A white lower-class Catholic woman saw the convent as one step up, and entering the seminary—particularly a Jesuit seminary—as another upward move.

My family was proud of my move; this was what they had hoped for. At the same time they were also resentful, for each step leads me away from them, makes me different. And the pain of being different from those whom I am most like runs very deep. I see further costs in terms of the women with whom I hope to work. Recently I called out to a woman of the streets, "Have a good night." Barely had the words left my lips when the expression on her face let me know that having a good night was not an option for her. What was good about the scavenger hunt for food and a place to rest? What was good about the fear of being picked up off the streets and taken to Boston State Hospital? She spoke no words, but I knew by her glare. And I wondered at the costs of upward mobility, at the price I was paying for my theological education, and felt the pain of knowing I would have to build bridges now to reach my people.

An upper-middle-class woman describes her journey:

Raised in a Catholic-Protestant family in the South, I knew the privileges of the white Southern lady yet had those modified by a strong commitment to the Protestant work ethic and a sense of the importance of my social responsibility to those who were "less privileged" than I. Education broadened my context and

24

provided tools for stepping back from the intensity of emotion that inevitably crested when I began to take parental and school guidelines concerning social justice and the injustice of inequality quite literally. This led to painful differences between me and my family, to my choosing to live differently than my family's means permitted, choosing to argue against a distribution of resources that provided me with the education and life-style which had led me here but at the expense of so many others. I do not seek to lower my standard of living but rather to raise the standard of living of others, knowing that mine and my family's must change if this is to happen. I cannot walk away from the privilege I inherit. It is manifest in how I move in the world, from how I say hello, to how I run a board meeting or set the table. It gives me access to people in power who might listen to one of their own.

Growing knowledge of my class privilege had enhanced my awareness of myself as oppressor and had increased my sense of the need to act concretely in ways that manifest my choice for different values, my struggle for a different system which guarantees that basic human needs for food, clothing, shelter, education, and health care will be met. But it has also deepened the rift between me and my family.

Another Southern perspective completes our group's story:

My family roots are Southern working class, evangelical Protestant. Education was seen as the key to upward mobility. Even though upward mobility was valued, affluence was not. I learned a strong sense of fair play and bias in favor of the underdog as examples of Christian virtue. College, for me, became not only a vehicle for upward mobility, but a politicizing experience, transforming those individualized virtues into a social/political context and opening me up to understanding oppression and injustice.

Having shared these stories, group members tried to articulate the recurring themes, the insights that might, in turn, enhance understanding and inform future experiences. For all group members, education has been a critical factor. It has led to movement on the class ladder, but not without high costs. Everyone recognized the extent to which, whatever the costs, she now belonged to an educational elite. Education has separated some from families and friends. It has given each a way of participating in a monopoly of knowledge and of educational resources. Yet, for women, the experience is a double bind, for this is not an unequivocal monopoly of knowledge. Educated women have access to resources that such education provides, but they have also been excluded from the creation of these same thought systems and ideologies. In many ways, particularly in theology and in the history of Western religious thought, women have been defined out of existence. Hence our appropriation of this knowledge has carried with it a critique of its method and its content (see chapter 1 for further elaboration). How, concretely, do we act in response to this insight?

Each of us has acted and continues to act in relationship to family and friends. We have also felt the need to seek a broader context for understanding the function of our education, to analyze its role in our society. We are being and have been educated in the ways of Western imperial patriarchal religion. Our schools of theology embrace this tradition and call it "universal truth." Our churches support them in this process. In addition, our schools and churches are in communities where they have an impact on the economy. Thus we need to examine the economic relationship between our schools and the local community, the impact of vast amounts of tax-free property on a budget of a local community, and hence on the quality of the services it can provide, to name but one example.

In our discussion we attempted to distinguish class from status, privilege, and caste. Classic Marxist doctrine defines social class in terms of one's relationship to ownership of the means of production. William Ryan, drawing on the work of Max Weber and C. Wright Mills, has defined class as referring to "economic ranking, to the possession and control of wealth and the sources of wealth, and to relative advantage in the marketplace."[1] Other commentators on Marx have sought to clarify the differences between class, status, and caste, and to distinguish between the stratification that results from each. Status relates more to prestige and social honor, and caste relates to biological or hereditary traits. Both are distinguished from class, which has to do with economic reality.

With this working definition we must return to an examination of our family stories and our present experience as theological students, teachers, and ministers. We have begun the analysis at the individual level and have hinted at its implications for an understanding of the class bias of our theological education and of much of the church. Such analyses must be pressed by women in theological education; otherwise the elitism and the exclusivity of a class system that alienates and oppresses so many of our sisters and brothers will be blindly perpetuated.

Sexuality

Sexual identity/sexuality was a difficult topic to approach and address openly throughout the consultation. Only during the final sessions did it become apparent to all the participants that what was happening within this group constituted a microcosm of the current situation of people in the church and in society in general. We had experienced a sense of comfort and confidence rising from a common goal that allowed us to articulate a diversity of opinions concerning the direction and strategies we wished to take in theological education. We had failed, however, explicitly to identify and effectively to discuss one subject that continues

27

to have a profound impact on all the other areas of our lives; namely, our sexual identity as women and the powerful presence of sexuality in our lives.

Why do we have this difficulty? The concept of sexuality has been fragmented and, to some extent, straitjacketed into some distinct categories. This fragmentation encourages discussions about family life, heterosexuality, homosexuality, and celibacy that lead to a diffusion of the tremendous power inherent in the sexual, as experienced in common by all. This force, although it often goes unnamed, leads us to seek communion with others and the myriad possibilities for good that are inherent in meaningful relationships. Its influence extends beyond the personal to the sociopolitical, the theological, and the ethical.

A tension presents itself as we seek to identify for ourselves who we are as women. Untold generations of women have taken the dominant white male definition of woman as their own. A woman is wife, mother, sister, whore. She is nurturer, "the heart," caretaker of emotion, as well as nag and bitch. She is *not* assertive, aggressive, capable of independence, or capable of holding positions of authority and power. She represents the sexual and is therefore tainted and evil. When we struggle to claim *a view of ourselves* that abolishes the dualism inherent in the dominant definition, that integrates our minds and bodies, we face centuries of opposition stemming from this false dichotomy.

Christian identity emerged and the earliest theologies developed in an era that was steeped in a cultural understanding of humanity that made sharp distinctions between the spiritual and the material, the mind and the body, male and female. Platonic, Neoplatonic, and Manichaeistic philosophies, as well as classical literature, were the basis for this understanding in the Roman world. The senses were continually at war with reason, enticing,

28

tempting, threatening the way to a purer/otherworldly existence and thus to perfection.

To one degree or another, most of the early Christian writers shared a negative view of woman as the embodiment of the sexual (and thus the *uncontrollable*), and it has been successfully transmitted through the ages to the present. This influence remains pervasive throughout society. These tensions influence the directions we, as women, choose, the programs and curricula we develop, the relationships we have with the institutions with which we are affiliated. We are aware of endless possibilities and of a number of problems as well. A few examples from our experience in theological education may help to make this discussion more concrete.

Earlier we spoke of women being placed in the role of nurturer. It follows that women can easily relate to a return of a genuine notion of "ministry as service." This concept has been abused by a male model that has often used ministry as a vehicle for power and control. A woman who enters a self-defined ministry of service runs the risk of becoming a scapegoat, a servant, and a slave for those who have authority over her; it is argued that women are *expected* to be service/giving oriented. Again, when addressing those in administration, or confronting individuals concerning women's agenda, women are expected to understand and to sympathize with the problems of the institution and of the individual men when there is a conflict of needs. Thus, she is to assume the role of the "problemless problem-solver."

Conversely, women-identified women—women who have rejected male definitions of who they are or should be, who are comfortable with authority, who believe that power is good and can be used in the empowerment of others—are accused of *abandoning* a "ministry of service."

There have been some tentative ventures within our schools of theology to explore the question of sexuality.

29

Some women's organizations have dealt with the area of sexuality through the sponsorship of conferences and courses. For the past two years the Women's Theological Coalition (WTC) of the Boston Theological Institute (BTI), in conjunction with the Andover Newton Theological School Women's Resource Center, has sought to address the issue of lesbian women in the church, through the sponsoring of one weekend conference each year. While the conferences have been successful at raising the issue to the level of discussion and sharing, they suffer from a lack of broad-based constituency support. Furthermore, they have been met with a hostile reception from a number of students, both male and female. Resistance, however, has not reached the level of outright confrontation. In addition, such programs tend to raise the level of consciousness around these issues but often fail to develop concrete strategies for confronting oppression or for enabling *all* people to live integrated lives.

During the TWFM course at Andover Newton one year, a work group chose to address itself to the topic of sexuality and life-style. However, when the topic was subsequently presented to the entire class, the relevant issues were not addressed head-on. While the class presentation succeeded in engendering discussion about sexual awareness, the participants were not challenged to confront their individual assumptions and prejudices, nor to consider the impact of these on the dynamics of the group. As a result, the discussion developed with marriage as the assumed norm, failing to deal with the life-styles of single women or of lesbians. Furthermore, the underlying tension between lesbians and heterosexual participants was never resolved.

SQAG is a good example of a program that sought to deal with sensuality in its various manifestations but failed explicitly to confront the reality of homosexuality and its impact on the structure and the process of SQAG's programming. To its credit, it sought to create an atmosphere that supported physical, intellectual, and spiritual growth. Access to resources for athletics, for the arts, for study, and for worship, as well as explicit structuring of time to encourage such work and play, created an atmosphere that enabled wholistic education. As in the case of TWFM, consideration was given to the different life-style options and various sexual preferences of those who shared in the program. Because participants lived together in shared quarters there was also ample opportunity for personal sharing on these issues, and some myths and prejudices were exposed and explored by getting to know women who had chosen to love women. However, even in this open atmosphere, there remained painful elements of homophobia.

As a program, SQAG was unable to clarify its own position or to articulate in an explicit way an understanding of homosexuality/heterosexuality. Hence, despite the desire to deal openly with issues of life-style, it perpetuated a silence that serves to separate women from one another. Unfortunately, this silence supports a mystification of, a fear of, and an oppression of lesbian bonding between women. Some women who have attempted to understand lesbiansim as a viable alternative life-style have felt hindered by the absence of visible role models. Society, in general, offers no affirmation, and the institutional church neither blesses nor celebrates the choice. In fact, it frequently condemns any homosexual life-style and has little sympathy for the personal struggle involved.

Both black and Hispanic women may have particular difficulty in exploring alternative life-styles since, from their particular cultural perspectives, the value of the family and of the female/male relationship is closely linked to their racial heritage. Thus, to question their conception of family may necessitate the questioning of their heritage. To choose lesbianism, then, has different implications for racial minority women than for white women.

31

The lesbian, a woman who has chosen to share her most intimate self in an explicitly sexual way with another woman, is experienced by many as the ultimate threat. To men, she, of all women, is the one who, by her very definition as lesbian, offers no willingness to enter into an intimate relationship wherein the man may be the dominant figure. Any desire on the part of man, whether conscious or unconscious, to assert his supremacy in the intimate realm of physical relationship meets with frustration in the case of the lesbian. To her heterosexual sisters she may also pose a threat, leading them to question the extent to which they, in their personal lives, are truly woman-identified. In the eyes of the heterosexual woman who is struggling to maintain a balanced relationship with the man or men with whom she is intimately involved, the lesbian may consciously or unconsciously introduce another element of tension.

What happens when a seminary group running a program becomes lesbian-identified? Part of the answer lies in *who* does the identifying. One group may make a corporate decision to take an active advocacy position, consciously choosing to become lesbian-identified, even though this position may not be reflected in the personal life-styles of all the group members. Another group may be identified as lesbian by those outside its membership, while the group itself may take an educational or advocacy stance without an explicitly lesbian identification. In other words, it may choose to present the issue of lesbianism without incarnating it through its self-identification. Although their politics and strategies may differ, both groups may experience similar consequences for being thus identified. For example, constituency relationships may become strained, and there may be a sharp decrease in the number of women who will choose to take advantage of the services the program offers. This avoidance may, of course, result from a fear that they, too, will be labeled lesbian. In addition, funding may be jeopardized. In general, the funds for many women's programs are being cut off as seminaries reorient their budgets under a tighter fiscal fist. Under these conditions, administrators may have the perfect excuse they need to get themselves off the financial hook. Furthermore, such cuts may be more easily justified and more readily accepted by the academic community.

More positive outcomes of the above-mentioned lesbian identification are possible. Because of their visible stance, the first group may succeed in breaking new ground in the public's consciousness. This would include not simply clarifying an understanding of lesbianism as a life-style chosen by some. In addition, there would be a greater likelihood that others would begin to examine how they deal with the sexual in their own lives, regardless of their orientation. The educative position of the second group, however, is less confrontative and could therefore be less threatening. At the very least, it offers a place to begin examining the issues.

Finally, regardless of one's sexual orientation, it is necessary for all women in theological education to continue to examine our sexual identity and our lived experience of the sexual. To the extent that we consciously reach out to reclaim this power for our own, we will be able to bring a new wholeness to the fragmentation of persons still evident in the church and in society.

Exclusion/Inclusion

Issues of exclusion and inclusion are critical to our understanding of the questions related to constituency. The question of who we are, whether spoken or nonverbally understood, is central for all our groups. In determining who will form the constituency, the answers to this question shape the organization's direction, deciding which issues will be tackled and what approaches will be taken. Assumptions, principles, and actions are all encapsulated in the words, "Who are we?"

Neither exclusion nor inclusion, by definition itself, carries a value. Depending on the intent and the effect, either can be a positive or a negative force in an organization's development. Generally, exclusion can be either by design, as a strategy or goal, or by default. Sometimes it is the product of a group's myopic vision that tends to see only reproductions of itself: people are sought who are similar to the core membership, with differing approaches being either denied or demeaned. Exclusion may be unavoidable—and sometimes even desirable. However, it is important to distinguish different kinds of exclusion, between positions which must, of necessity, exclude people, and that form of exclusion which is caused by a group's inability or unwillingness to struggle with the implications of diversity. Perhaps one way to visualize a more positive model of exclusion/inclusion, one which is deliberate yet flexible, is to imagine a circle of changing size, sometimes continuous and sometimes with openings, that is always conscious of other circles and is, on occasion, continuous with them.

The reasons for exclusion are many. When one feels like a stranger in a dominant culture, a support group with a similar vision helps her/him not to feel isolated, "crazy," or impotent. However it is achieved, a shared perspective is essential. Moreover, meaningful programming must be specific if it is to have an impact. Persons respond most effectively and passionately to what they know. It is difficult to confront, let alone articulate, what has not been directly experienced. One's particular struggle has an immediacy not evoked by other concerns.

One question that does arise, even with "necessary" exclusion, is how to communicate, if at all, with "the other." "The other" may be translated as a dominant group (for example, women seminarians in relationship to the school's administration) or as another group struggling for rights (for example, feminists in relationship with those engaged in Third World liberation struggles). In creating "a woman's space," "a gay space," or "a black space," is there any responsibility to translate the reasons to those excluded? If so, how can this be done without expending superfluous energy? If not, is the group deliberately signaling that any attempt at communication will be counterproductive?

Whether exclusion is intentional or unconscious, one danger is that divisions established by the dominant society are adopted. Various groups on the "outside" of the decision-making view one another with mistrust and fight among themselves for a piece of the pie. The basic questions, such as how power can be redefined or how differences affect common efforts, remain unasked. Too often a stance of "progressiveness" or "radicalness" masks a need to be included in the system, even when its white, male middle-class orientation is contrary to the welfare of most people in the world.

Many women erroneously attempt to see feminism as apart from, if not indifferent to or threatened by, larger liberation struggles. Thus, individual egocentrism, fears, and prejudices are brought to the women's movement. Theological education also reinforces blindness to oppression. Christianity, as a Western patriarchal religion with an understanding of a God who works through history by taking sides, is often conceptualized in warlike language and images. Christians often refuse to recognize how particular religious institutions rip off the community through real estate transactions, employment policies, or stock investments. It is not easy for a person to admit that he/she benefits from oppression, or that there are many ways in which he/she may be the oppressor: as American, as white, as the black bourgeoisie, as middle class (in values and options, if not always in income), as theologians participating in a "monopoly of knowledge," or as an ordained elite. Too often persons who have these "advantages" cling to them and fail to realize the far greater needs of the millions who are starving and homeless. As a result, the focus and impact of change efforts are narrowed, contradictions are avoided, and "society" is called upon to change, while those in positions of relative power play it "safe," and in the process lose sight of the interconnectedness of liberation struggles.

And so, feeling the burden of our exclusivity yet recognizing its limited merits, we at the consultation wrestled with how our groups had sometimes destructively and other times wisely defined our constituency and our programs. In summary, many of us had overlooked the richness which, for example, seminary staff, nonfeminists, evangelicals, and working-class people might bring to our efforts. Many times groups needlessly carried a label such as "white" or "Protestant."

We spoke of what it's like to feel outside an alternative organization: one seminarian talked of being Catholic in the predominantly Protestant Women's Theological Coalition. A member of the Women's Counseling Team shared how that organization found itself fighting against black students over a faculty appointment at Union Theological Seminary; it was too late when some began to question why only one position was open and to challenge the method being used in filling it. BWIM discussed the difficulties as well as the excitement of developing programming for a constituency that spans decades; represents faiths as varied as Pentecostal, Catholic, and Presbyterian; encompasses both nonfeminist and feminist understanding; and includes both the formally educated and the life-tutored. A SQAG representative explored how the organization's location, alternative programming, and feminist and post-Christian dimension had in the past limited, if not excluded, racial minority groups and low-income women.

A representative from TWFM criticized the ways in which racism had unconsciously affected TWFM's hiring practices and had constricted its relationships with black students.

Through these discussions, as we attempted clarification, our task as feminists became more complex. Questions were raised that eluded ready answers. We challenged ourselves to recognize the uneasy tension arising between those sharing a particular affinity and those outside. Realizing that no facile either/or solution exists, we were attempting to become conscious of the times we view others as "them," and how often we are the oppressors as well as the oppressed. Hence, the issue of inclusion or of exclusion is one aspect of constituency that affects the ways in which we make concrete through our programs our understandings of race, class, and sexuality.

CHAPTER 3

Racism and the Responsibilities of White Women in Theological Education

A major problem in developing women's programs is the extent to which we mirror the dominant system, perpetuating much of what we critique in that system. Racism is a prime example of this problem. In describing our programs, we clearly identify racism as an issue that must be addressed:

> Of the 550 women in the B.T.I. schools, 15 are black. How to support these women and how to deal with our own racism (and class biases) are perhaps the most serious problems we face.
>
> Women's Theological Coalition
> Boston Theological Institute

> From its inception the program has sought to address the needs and reflect the reality of ethnic women of color as well as white women.
>
> Research/Resource Associates Program
> Harvard Divinity School

> Among the basic assumptions [of SQAG] is that sexism cannot be understood apart from race and class and vice versa.
>
> Seminary Quarter at Grailville

Some major themes and issues [are] racism and heterosexism.
Women Counseling Team
Union Theological Seminary

As these programs have been developed, there has been a clear race-consciousness and a recognition that issues of racism must be addressed in and by women's programs. Yet, as close examination of the programs represented by participants in this consultation reveals, racism persists—a clear indication that race-consciousness does not in itself eliminate racism.

The reason that racism persists in spite of our good intentions becomes clear as we articulate our understanding of racism as a white problem which functions within the ordinary "way-of-being" in white society. Because this is true, a passive response that overlooks or ignores the issue perpetuates the racism of the culture.[1] This is no less true in predominantly white seminaries than in the larger society. Thus it is crucial that we examine our assumptions and clarify our definitions of racism.

In doing so it is important to make a distinction between racism and some other often confused concepts, such as prejudice, bigotry, and discrimination. While these three terms reflect attitudes and behaviors that may be symptomatic of racism, they are more general terms and don't necessarily involve access to and use of power in the way racism does.[2] Racism is understood as a system of attitudes, behaviors, and assumptions that objectifies human persons on the basis of color, and that has the power to deny autonomy, access to resources, and self-determination to those persons, while maintaining the values of the dominant society as the norm by which all else will be measured. Although these systems are creations of the social order, they come to be seen as "natural." Racism takes personal, institutional, and cultural forms and operates at intentional and unintentional, overt and covert levels. Thus

39

the elimination of racism requires a continual reexamination of our cultural assumptions, institutional policies, and personal attitudes.

When programs controlled by white women are examined in this light, too often patterns reflecting the images of racism become apparent—white women designing programs to address the "needs of women" as though the needs as defined by white women are applicable to all women. In this way the norms are established by which all else will be judged:

—Some funds (however small) are controlled by white women who are often more willing to fund programs of white women than those of racial minority women because they understand the former better.

—When black women develop space to address issues of particular concern to black women, they are accused of "reverse" racism, and the burden of building bridges is placed on black women.

—Hiring policies are established that result in hiring only one, if any, racial minority woman in a multiple staff program, perpetuating the unspoken and unexamined assumptions (e.g., regarding numbers and salary of staff) of the dominant system.

—History is written without reference to the issue of racism or to the participation of racial minority women, perpetuating white definitions of reality by "overlooking" the problem of racism.

—Programs are planned by white women who consult with one black woman, objectifying her and using her as a "resource," while continuing to define the needs of the program (e.g., research, ministry) in terms of the assumptions of white models.

—Programs are designed in such a way that the structure itself is more open to white than black women. For example, "self-directed learning" programs, when predominantly white, tend to define "needs" in terms of white women's concerns.

As we have examined our work, we have become aware again of the depth of the racism in our culture and the extent to which we must give attention to its elimination if we are to develop programs and structures that address the needs and concerns of all women.[3]

We must begin this process by taking responsibility for our own racism. It is symptomatic of the racism of our society that we often try to place the blame somewhere else—on the institutions to which we are attached or on the obvious bigots who make the news. We have been allowed to do this because we are part of the dominant culture that has the power to define, and we have learned to define the cause of racism as "somebody else." But this is not an adequate response. Only if we can say the "I"—"I am a racist"—will we be able to move beyond a liberalism that adopts the language of equality but maintains the structure of oppression. Accepting such responsibility requires that we develop ways for coping with racism within and among ourselves. Too often white women ask black women to come into a white program to deal with the "racial problem," implying that racism is a black problem, to be solved by blacks. Such attempts misplace the problem and give white women an "out."

The importance of this beginning point is especially relevant in two programs we have examined—Training Women for Ministry and Seminary Quarter at Grailville. Both programs are designed on a self-directed learning model. Our experiences with these programs have made us aware of some contradictons between attempting to address racism and the self-directed model. Many times white women intellectualize the issue of racism as something we "study" in ethics courses, whereas in

41

self-directed learning settings we deal with *our* concerns (the implication being that racism is not *our* problem). Self-directed learning, because it is more experiential, moves away from the objective study approach and provides a setting that has potential for addressing racism in a more immediate sense, especially if the group is multiracial and/or there are white women present who have been able to say the "I" to own their racism and to push other white women to do so too. However, even this approach does not overcome the racism of the culture; indeed, it is precisely that culture which allows white women to say that racism is not *our* concern. Consequently, race-conscious white participants often adopt typically liberal language of equality and assume, therefore, that the problem has been solved. The reality of the issue is then ignored, and white women thereby become allies of those in power, failing to understand how racism affects their lives.

This failure raises the question of self-interest. What is the self-interest for white women in combating racism? One of the results of the way racism functions is that while liberal whites in the society are able to recognize some of the negative consequences such a system has on the lives of racial minority persons, they are not able to recognize the negative consequences for white persons. These consequences—a distorted ethnocentric view of the world, a limited understanding of ourselves and our history, a sense of competitiveness that motivates us to stay "on top"; in short, a lack of freedom and wholeness which results from participating in a system that denies these qualities to others—are hidden behind the facade of privilege and the myth of cultural superiority.

So, when we examine self-directed learning programs, we are faced with the problem of how to maintain the important dimension of empowerment and self-confidence which can be built through such programs without having them become one more place that protects white women from dealing with the reality of racism.

The emphasis on beginning with our own racism also raises a key theological issue. Many of us are afraid to acknowledge that all whites—even those who haven't been "bad" (i.e., even those who disavow racism), by virtue of living in this culture and having access to the privileges which go with a white skin—are racist. The reason is that such a general statement seems to imply that change or repentance—"being good"—is impossible (since disavowing racism does not eliminate it). However, a deeper examination of the situation broadens our understanding of the connection between societal change and individual repentance. Even though I, as an individual, own my racism and think I am working with others to eliminate it in myself and the society, I still do not totally overcome it. Yet I can continue to work on the issue, recognizing that my work does not depend on my being free from sin (in this case, racism) but on my commitment to change. A theology of individual sin and individual salvation prevents us from addressing the systemic issues, because it implies that if we "repent" (recognize the evils caused by racism and sincerely want change), we can claim to be nonracist (individual salvation results from individual repentance). To make such a claim denies the systemic reality (which, theologically speaking, involves corporate sin and corporate salvation), and in so doing short-circuits any steps we might make toward lasting change.

It is in the context of acknowledging our own racism that we can begin to understand the relationship between racism and sexism and how both function in theological education. Key to this understanding is the recognition of the position of white women as both the oppressed (in relation to white men) and the oppressors (in relation to racial minority communities).[4] The most obvious result of this has to do with access to resources: white male power structures set up white women and racial minority persons to fight with each other over resources controlled by white men. At the same time, any funds that are allocated for women's concerns are controlled by white women, with the result that funds are used to address the concerns of white women. Another result has to do with how white women define feminist issues. Too often this takes place in such a way that racial minority women can participate only at the expense of being alienated from their communities. For example, when abortion is discussed only in relation to the issue of choice, without giving consideration to issues of forced sterilization and genocide, the reality of racism is ignored. The issue is, therefore, worked on in such a way that "solutions" apply only to white women. Both alienation of racial minority women from their communities and the ethnocentric understanding of feminist issues are examples of how racism persists even in the midst of programs that have stated intentions of combating racism.

Two important issues need to be remembered in dealing with the oppressed/oppressor position of white women. The first is a question of loyalties: Where are we when the pinch comes? With whom do we identify? Historically, white middle-class women have identified with white middle-class men—no matter how much we fight against it—because we need to be included. Thus, traditional racist policies and practices are woven into white women's programs. The second is the extent to which we buy into the illusion of power—fighting with racial minority persons over decisions that will, in any case, be made by white men.

The relevance of these factors is seen in all our programs. Particular learnings have come from the difficulties that have arisen from time to time in the distribution of funds. In the Women's Theological Coalition, white women control a small amount of program money. Black women who wish to plan programs that address their needs and concerns must justify their program to white women. This very process tends toward paternalism (we do something for them if they are good) and therefore creates tensions and distrust, so that the potential for building alliances between the groups is jeopardized, if not destroyed.

Questions are raised here about future directions: How do we lift up and appreciate diversity without perpetuating the concept of "the other" who cannot be trusted? How do we develop new structures which involve both black and white women in controlling funds designated for women without demanding that black women join with white women on white women's terms? How do we develop strategies of cooperation between white women and racial minority persons so that we do not get caught in the trap of fighting with each other? The connections between racism and sexism are clear when liberal white men accuse women's programs of racism and black programs of sexism, while the institutions they control go on in the usual racist, sexist manner, objectifying both racial minority persons and white women, and denying us all access to resources and the power of self-determination and autonomy.

The allocation of funds and the power of white women has also been an issue in the Training Women for Ministry program and the Women Counseling Team with regard to hiring staff. In the former, tension was created between the program and black women in the Boston theological community because of the established policies, which were (1) that women already on the staff (all white) would continue if they wished (i.e., not be subject to review and rehiring procedures) and (2) that the number on the staff could not be expanded. These policies were adhered to, even though the result was that several excellent black candidates were rejected and only one was hired to be part of a three-person team. In the case of WCT, also a multiple staff program, the program existed for five years before there were any black women on the staff. In both instances the question of how to guard against structures that institutionalize racism is raised. The need to develop procedures for reviewing and keeping open our hiring policies is clear if we are to avoid the racist practices used by the dominant institution to maintain white males in jobs and positions of power.

The Research/Resource Associates Program has had a related problem. Although there has been participation of black women since its inception, the history of this program clearly reveals that the move from developing inclusive structures within our own programs to confronting systemic racism is long and difficult. Here we see an example of the contradiction between race-consciousness and combating racism. The emphasis has been on race—hiring a black candidate as an associate—while the definitions of research and need have remained unchanged. Because the program exists within an institution that defines research in such a narrow way as to cut it off from the black church as a source for learning history, theology, homiletics, and ethics, the work of black associates is seen as peripheral to the real business of theological education, and often as peripheral to the concerns of white women who have internalized the system's definitions of the "basics." The relationship between racism and sexism is particularly clear in this setting: the program itself is token for women. Therefore, white women, oppressed by the dominant institution, are put into an oppressor role when they accept the institution's definition of reality. Again we are faced with the necessity of change in structures of power, definitions of reality, and access to resources if we are to move beyond tokenism to systemic change.

A related question faced by the Women's Theological Coalition connects as well to the issue mentioned earlier of how the needs of white women are defined. It is important that we not only address the structural relationships of power and control in the distribution of funds among racial minority women and white women, but also that we

46

examine the ways program funds are used *by* white women *for* white women. What are the priorities (i.e., where are we willing to put our time, energy, and money) when we attempt to address feminist concerns? Are we willing to put them into understanding and dealing with our own racism?

This is particularly difficult when we are confronted with a problem which is so pervasive that white people have learned how to live with it without seeing it. Consequently, the assumption is that we are dealing with an issue that only exists in situations in which there are significant numbers of racial minority persons (another example of misplacing the problem). The extent to which we, as white women, adopt the practices of the dominant system is seen also when we write our stories (our history), neglecting to mention racism as an issue. While white participants in both the WCT and the Center for Women and Religion articulate the need for addressing issues of racism and classism as well as sexism, the histories of those programs are written without reference to either the participation of racial minority women or the ways racism is addressed among white women. Again we are confronted with the need to continue to work on ways to guard against our own racism—as reflected here in ignoring or overlooking the problem—recognizing that we are both products and perpetuators of a racist system.

The examination of our history makes our complicity painfully clear, both in perpetuating racism in the structures over which we have some control, and also in our failure to effect change in those institutions to which we are attached.

However, it would be an incomplete picture to look only at the points of failure. Most programs have also experienced points of breakthrough, as program participants have been open to learning from mistakes. Two examples involving internal structural change are:

47

—The Seminary Quarter at Grailville is in the process of developing new directions based on a realization that its structure and location, over the last four years, has not had a wide appeal among racial minority women. Black women and white women who have participated in the program are in the process of planning urban-based programs for the future. It is intended that the redesigned program will give attention to maintaining the values of the self-directed model, while at the same time building-in a variety of structural dimensions to address issues of racism among white women and content areas of particular concern to black women (preaching, biblical interpretation, community-organizing in black perspective).

—The Women's Theological Coalition is in the process of reexamining its structure to deal with the inequity in control over funds and has also set aside time and program money for workshops in which white women can work on racism, both in its individual dimensions and in its institutional and cultural dimensions.

Throughout the programs there are indications of individual and collective commitments to work toward eliminating racism. There are evidences of changed attitudes and structures, and the development of new programs that recognize the connection between racism and sexism—all of which give validity to the theological claim mentioned earlier, that change *can* take place in the midst of sin, and that commitments for continued transformation from oppression toward liberation are possible.

CHAPTER 4

Marginality, Alternative Structures, and Leadership Styles

It is a tenet of liberation theology that who we are makes a difference in how we theologize. The new constituencies discussed in chapter 2 are raising new theological questions out of life experiences. In the last six years women have become the fastest growing constituency in American theological schools. The Association of Theological Schools' *Fact Book on Theological Education* reports that 8,972 women were enrolled in 193 schools in the United States and in Canada in 1978, making up nearly 20% of the total student body. One half of the 2,200 new students entering seminary in the fall of 1978 were women. The greatest increase in numbers has been among the women in programs leading to ordination: their numbers have increased by 269.6% between 1972 and 1978, ten times greater than among men.

Black students—men and women—are 4.1% of the grand total of 46,460 theological students. Among the women seminary students, only 298 (about 3%) are black, and another 89 (less than 1%) are Hispanic.

Marginality—A Fact of Life

Despite our rapid increase in numbers, women are latecomers to the seminary scene and remain marginal to the system, a fact made clear in countless ways. According to the Association of Theological Schools' *Fact Book,* women constitute about 10% of the persons now teaching in seminaries. On closer examination, however, these figures tend to overstate the case. Of the 471 women faculty listed, 301 (or 64%) are part-time; only 27 are full professors. For example, the Graduate Theological Union numbers 400 women among its 1,100 students; of the 175 persons on the faculty, 6 are women; none is tenured. The Boston Theological Institute, which boasts the largest group of women seminarians in the world— 650 women—has 53 women faculty, about half of whom are full-time; only 3 are tenured. Part-time appointments are one way of keeping women marginal to the institution: a woman may be hired to teach a single course or invited as a visiting lecturer for an academic year or quarter, and in that capacity has no voice in institutional policies or decision-making. In one case a woman with a fine record as a successful teacher was given a permanent appointment "without right of review," in effect making her appointment permanent but nontenured, so that she would not qualify to sit on key faculty committees. Some schools go through the motions of interviewing women for new openings, but search committees have been known to reach a decision before they have conducted the interviews with the women applicants. Women's studies courses are kept to a very small part of the turf; they may be given only once, usually are avoided by male students, and rarely become part of the standard curriculum.

In administration, women are similarly cribbed, cabined, and confined. While 15.9% of the seminary administrators are women, the largest number of women in administrative posts (63, or 58%) are registrars, a record-keeping rather than a policy-making role. No school has a woman in the top administrative position; only four schools have women in assistant or associate positions. The position of coordinator of women's programs is often established on an ad hoc basis, with a vague and all-encompassing job description that can later be quietly undermined. Sometimes other jobs are added to the coordinator's portfolio—"Would you mind taking on the work of the registrar?"—until she has no time left for programming or for advocacy.

Financially, the programs are clearly marginal, being funded almost without exception on some special basis: by outside funding, which means that the program is cut when the funding comes to an end; or by "special funds," which can easily be cut when budgets tighten up; or by special grants, which entail multiple fund-raising campaigns. It is rare to find a women's program as a line item in a seminary budget. The short-term, catch-as-catch-can funding pattern takes a heavy toll in staff time, energies, and anxieties. At the same time, the institutions tend to take full credit for the programs they support inadequately or not at all—"Look at all the special resources and services we provide for our women!"—and they tend to use any advances that have been made as an excuse for not doing anything further; for example, some seminaries regard Seminary Quarter at Grailville as providing a women's studies program for their students.

Underlying the other experiences of marginality is the strong sense of exclusion from the real decision-making process. "We make reports that no one reads" . . . "Hours of work on committees evaluating programs and negotiating with all involved parties are not attended to in faculty meetings" . . . "We have access to some formal decision-making bodies, but the real decisions are made either in the formal structures in which we have no voice or 'in the old boys' club.' " Women in the seminary structures are still the outsiders, not "in-the-know," suppliants looking for crumbs of vital information; and women's programs lead a precarious existence on the boundaries of the institutions.

51

Some Effects of Marginality on Women

The overcommitment generally characteristic of feminist enterprises appears to hold true among the feminists in theology. Because people are acting out of deep personal convictions, they tend to try to meet all the diverse demands made on them—demands to speak at programs and conferences, to sit on committees, to join networks, to write articles, to take action on behalf of some individual case or united front. Women in coordinator or advocacy roles within the seminaries tend to overextension almost by job definition. Many positions that are defined as half-time outline a task which would require at least two full-time people for even moderate coverage. Consulting with faculty and administrators, doing long-range planning, writing funding proposals and keeping contact with possible funding sources, working with a steering committee or board, organizing and supervising a student staff, guiding projects to approval through the arcane political processes of academe—little wonder that a person struggling to get through such an agenda in two and a half days a week may feel exhausted after a year or two. As a matter of fact, there is a high turnover in coordinator positions; seldom does any individual stay more than two years, a circumstance that makes it difficult to maintain continuity. Rarely does the organization take full advantage of the experience and insights of the person who is leaving, to reexamine its structures and ways of working. Systematic feedback from the departing staff person might result in more realistic goal statements and job descriptions.

A second consequence of marginality is that the institution tends to put the new organization on the defensive. The burden of proof is on the innovators to establish the validity of their work. At best, the institution ignores the marginal enterprise; at worst, it criticizes the program for "not integrating itself into the seminary"—an obvious example of blaming the victim. The underlying assumption of such criticisms is that the present educational system is in good health, and that any call for change must justify itself.

Overexhaustion and living on the defensive are obvious consequences of marginality for faculty and staff of women's programs; however, there is a much more subtle and far-reaching deformation of women's consciousness implicit in the content, structures, and methods of seminary education that affects students as well. The content, like academic content in other disciplines, almost entirely ignores the existence and contributions of women. When it does consider women, it does so out of the misogynism of the Jewish and Christian traditions, identifying women with the flesh, temptation, and sin. At best, women are regarded as objects of inquiry, not as the originators of intellectual or spiritual works. When women attempt to raise questions and pursue research in the areas of their concern, they find themselves entangled in a web of obstacles. A doctoral candidate's committee refuses to accept research into the work of women in the Methodist Church in the nineteenth century as a suitable topic for a dissertation; a dean insists that a doctoral committee of three women and one man is unbalanced and adds two men to it; women students are told that they may submit their study of a woman theologian for their comprehensive examinations *if* this work is in addition to the five (male) theologians that are already required, and on and on. Women regularly find themselves in the position of having to pursue their major concern in their spare time. Some women react to this situation by dropping out altogether; others allow themselves to be co-opted by the system and avoid women's issues as a subject of study in order to escape a debilitating struggle against charges of unscholarly subjectivity and emotionalism.

In short, a woman is apt to emerge from theological

53

education more or less alienated, laden with content that systematically ignores her own existence and downgrades her possibilities of achievement. Moreover, her intellectual style has been formed on a masculine model: objective, impersonal, abstract, oriented toward products rather than process, competitive, and elitist. Increasingly, knowledge is seen as a scarce good, not distributable but diminished by being shared; hence, the weary graduate students who hoard their ideas and live in fear lest someone may "steal" their thesis topics. What is at stake, of course, is not understanding or insight that is generated and increased in the process of open sharing, but the jobs, prestige, and status to which officially credentialed knowledge can lead in this society. These latter goods are indeed scarce—if I get the job, you don't; if I translate the newly discovered ancient manuscript, your translation will be a drug on the market; if I am first in the class, you can only be second.

But the intellectual style toward which women are tending is almost the opposite of this objective, competitive model. It attempts to bridge the gulf between objective and subjective, frankly recognizes and speaks from the "I," is open to the nonrational in human experience, is concerned with process as well as product, is contextual and interdisciplinary, flexible in method, collaborative in style, nonhierarchical and nonelitist, concerned with ways to share knowledge and skills rather than hoard expertise. For the learner who is trying to develop her intellectual strengths and skills, it is somewhat schizoid to attempt to acquire both these approaches at the same time. And it is a frustrating, energy-draining experience to have to fit one's real questions and concerns into the time left over from meeting external and uncongenial demands.

Alternative Spaces

The experience of marginality leads naturally to the search

for alternative spaces, spaces where women's concerns can be treated as central. The issue of autonomy is crucial—an alternative space is quite literally "a room of one's own," a space that women control both physically and psychologically. Usually, it involves a physical place—office center, house, farm—where the women involved can shape the environment to their liking in some significant degree. Always it involves the organizational right to set boundaries, to decide who may or may not participate or become members. Some alternative spaces are totally outside the university or seminary: an off-campus women's center; a place like Grailville, which is owned and operated by a women's group; a women's therapy collective; a house for battered women. Some are enclaves on the campus, given the use of a few rooms and scrambling to get together the necessary equipment. Whatever the concrete form, the one thing necessary is the institutionally recognized right to organize meetings, conferences, whatever, for women only. Even in those situations in which this right is "officially" recognized, the assumption of autonomy involved generally provokes predictable dynamics: either the puzzled protests of the excluded males—"How can they do this when they are drawing funds from our common budget?"—or a more or less anxious and threatened, "What are they up to? Are they planning something against us?" It is all reminiscent of the first white reactions to black power and black demands for separate centers and dormitories on the campuses of the 60s.

The meaning of alternative space has been understood somewhat differently by black women and white women. The programs developed by white women have their roots in the women's movement and draw their constituency largely from women in seminaries. In contrast, black women identify strongly with the black community; for example, the Black Women in Ministry (BWIM) program conceives of its alternative space as a natural response of a tiny minority (there are about twenty black women among the 2,000 students in the Boston Theological Institute) "to the present situation which has always been one of survival," and sees the roots of its work in the struggle of the black community for liberation. Out of this rooting in the black community, BWIM offers black women seminarians opportunities for mutual support, education, and advocacy, while emphasizing an inclusive membership that reaches beyond the seminary to pastors, spouses, teachers of Christian education, and laywomen generally.

Alternative spaces have a number of obvious advantages, realized more or less fully, depending on the investment of time and energy, and the degree of commitment of those involved. They provide opportunities for personal growth, for creativity and resource development, for a new learning process, for experiments with new structures and forms of action.

Nothing can take the place of being on one's own turf. If one has always been an outsider, it is almost impossible to imagine what it would feel like to be and to be affirmed as inside, as central. Grailville, as an educational center and farm owned and directed by women, makes a powerful impression on the participants in Seminary Quarter by the sheer fact of its being. "When I saw Judy riding the big tractor and doing the mowing, then it really struck me that I was in a women's place," one student reported. Grailville's function in setting a climate in which women are taken seriously is not unlike that of the women's colleges. One could call this the medium-is-the-message function of the alternative space. It is compounded of many unspoken assumptions, all the more powerful because taken for granted: that women are to be taken seriously and listened to with respect; that they are capable of achievements in all spheres; that women role models are an influential means of demonstrating the diverse ways of being a competent, compassionate human being.

The positive climate of the alternative space makes it a good environment for personal growth. The individual can relax, lower her defenses, get in touch with her own feelings, voice her pain and anger to sympathetic listeners, and thus begin a process of healing. The discovery that others have experienced similar sufferings, that personal pain is linked to systematic causes, that mutual trust and support are possible among women—all this is energizing and empowering. The freedom from the competitive environment and the defensiveness it provokes, together with the encouragement to trust one's own perceptions, makes it possible for new ideas to emerge, much as the thaws and sunshine of spring make it possible for the first green shoots to poke their heads above ground. A new intellectual climate and a new approach to learning—experience-based, collaborative, collegial, interdisciplinary, and wholistic—are able to emerge. Learning becomes a process of affirming rather than putting down the learner. In such a supportive environment one dares to claim one's questions, to think the hitherto unthinkable thought, to make the first tentative explorations into new territory.

The alternative spaces reviewed in this study have been successful in stimulating creativity and in developing new resources for women in theology. The women in Seminary Quarter report that ideas which first germinated at Grailville opened up topics for doctoral dissertations and plans for new ministries. The Harvard Research/Resource Associates Program and the Visiting Scholar Program at the Center for Women and Religion have brought about significant changes in personal growth, political and spiritual consciousness-raising, and the discovery of new areas of research and new methodologies within the theological disciplines. Both programs have produced courses, bibliographies, and research articles that serve as valuable resources, and have helped to develop women scholars and educators in religious studies. The Training

Women for Ministry program has demonstrated creativity in developing a new model for theological education and in enabling individual women to design new forms of ministry.

Finally, alternative spaces have given women an opportunity to experience leadership and to experiment with new forms of organization. This topic bulks so large in women's recent experience and writing that we want to consider it at some length.

The Search for Alternative Structures and Collective Styles

Women in theological education, like women in the movement generally, have been sharply critical of existing organizational structures, whether of the establishment or of the left, as power-mad, hierarchical, oppressive, fragmenting, bureaucratic, and elitist. Understandably, since women have abundant experience of being controlled by existing organizational structures, the early stages of the women's movement reacted strongly against all structures. Moreover, another factor was at work in this rejection; namely, the awareness that the medium *is* the message, that the process can negate the content, as, for example, tight control by the authoritarian teacher in the classroom negates the lesson about democratic values. Women have been determined not to fall into this trap, and thus, energies have been poured into a search for ways of working together that would embody our values.

The values sought have been variously named: to control one's own life, a concern for the development of each person, a concern with feelings as well as thought, open communication, community, sisterhood, the sharing of skills and responsibility. In the first phase of the endeavor to implement these values women emphasized the leaderless, structureless group as the ideal form of the movement.

No "stars" in the spotlight, no "elites" for us! The movement moved: consciousness-raising groups sprang up across the country almost overnight; women's centers appeared on campuses and in the cities; women's studies courses and programs multiplied like magic; the media moved in. Gradually, women began to discover that while unstructured interaction might work quite well for small, face-to-face consciousness-raising groups, it did not lend itself to the accomplishment of other tasks. Jo Freeman, in her article "The Tyranny of Structurelessness," pointed out that if a group refuses to name a spokesperson (to avoid "stars"), the media will do so, with two unhappy consequences: the group, not having named the speaker, cannot remove her; and the individual, thrown into the limelight willy-nilly, is often subjected to harsh, destructive criticism by her sisters. Many groups are finding that the refusal to set up explicit structures leads to immobilization, or to hidden and therefore nonaccountable leadership, or to elitist decision-making. At the present moment the movement appears to be passing from the celebration of structurelessness into a new phase, characterized by a search for non-oppressive structures.

For the present the key question seems to be: How can a group work as a collective without hierarchy but not without structure? Or better, since it is always dangerous to define oneself negatively: How can women form organizations in ways that affirm peer relationships and participative styles? The remainder of this chapter deals with the internal structures and dynamics of women's groups; chapter 5 deals with organizational styles and strategies as women work for institutional change.

The Search for Collective Styles

The following discussion is based on the programs reviewed in this book and on more general feminist analyses of power and organization. What, then, are the learnings from women's experiments with collectives about the ways to make collective styles work?

Perhaps the first essential is that a group come to terms with its ambivalences about power, leadership, and structures and be willing to accept these phenomena as inevitable aspects of any group.[1] The choice is not between power and no power, or structure and no structure, but between overt and covert, the explicit and the hidden structuring and use of power.

Second, a group must be able to identify and confront "the tyranny of the weak," a kind of power dynamic that seems especially prevalent in white women's groups. A person may have power by designation in virtue of a role she has agreed to fill; she may have power because of her special knowledge or skill; she may have power because of her maturity, the integration of her personality—what Maslow called self-actualization. The woman with a poor self-image, who sees herself as weak and worthless, often feels threatened in the presence of the strong, capable person. It is as though she sees power as limited: "If you are competent, I am lessened thereby." And she may resort to a double-bind strategy: either, "I'm a poor victim, here is my pain; you must rescue me, help me, hold back your strength"; or, "You refuse to rescue me, you go on threatening me, you are an insensitive, uncaring person." Using this victim game, the weakest person in a group may immobilize the stronger and more competent, and may even manipulate the entire group into the position of "Let's show our caring by all being weak together." Judith Bardwick offers the following analysis of this dynamic:

> Those who are easily manipulated by others who have more powerful roles or especially by others with stronger personalities are not likely to use direct or overt forms of aggression. They are more likely to be overtly fawning or ingratiating but

covertly and subtly aggressive. This form of attack makes it more difficult to label their intent as aggressive and to hold them responsible for their aggression. . . . The more powerful woman is likely to act supportively rather than assertively and the weaker has inhibited the stronger . . . . Since the emotional acting out is a plea for support by someone who shows her needs overtly, the needs are acknowledged but the aggressive manipulation is not and is, in fact, very difficult to see. After all, how many people are aware of the fact that when someone says, "I need you," they may also be saying, "I hate you." Not many.

If the group is without leadership, roles or tasks . . . it becomes quite possible for the emotionally demanding weaker women to dominate what occurs and thereby become the strongest members of the group.[2]

There are two ways a group can deal with this dynamic. First, it can learn to spot this subtle form of aggression and can hold the person responsible for her behavior. Second, it can reduce the level of threat to the weaker members by clear structuring of roles and delegation of authority. The more amorphous and unstructured the situation, the more the interactions tend to become a matter of interpersonal influence; hence, the higher the level of threat for the less confident members. Clear role definitions reduce this threat and increase the opportunities for equal participation.

Of course, clear delegations of authority presuppose a third essential for the collective; namely, that the group has dealt with such vital structural issues as the definition of its constituency, goals, priorities, requirements for membership, procedures for decision-making. Initially, in the name of openness, many groups allowed anyone who happened into a meeting to participate in decisions that affected the group. There is also the opposite problem—what about the person who clearly belongs to the group but does not attend decision-making meetings? Lots of rhetoric gets thrown up around this issue: "We don't want to compel anyone." "She is the best judge of her own needs." "But the group is not complete if she is not here." After a longer or shorter struggle many groups come out with a norm like: Participants are responsible to be at decision-making meetings or to communicate the reasons for their absence; and they are expected to abide by decisions reached in their absence. As a group takes on a demanding task, such as running a women's health center or a crisis phone line, it needs to develop a norm about doing its homework, since responsible decision-making requires substantial knowledge about the effects of policies, the outcomes of programs, the making of budgets, and other details of the group's work.

These considerations about membership point toward another structural need: some form of preparation or training for new members. The larger the group, the more necessary some fairly well-defined training period becomes.

The keystone of the structure is, of course, the procedure for decision-making. A group will need to deal with such questions as: What kinds of decisions do we need to make? Who will make them? Which decisions are matters for the total group? Which can be delegated? What procedures do we want to use? Do we want to work by consensus? By majority vote? By some combination of these? If we use majority vote, how do we ensure that the rights of the minority will be respected? What methods do we use to hold the decision-makers accountable?

In its day-to-day life a group needs to maintain a balance between task and maintenance, getting the job done and developing good relationships between the members. In the concern to give feelings their due, women's groups may fall into "the pit of process," in which all anyone needs to do to stop the proceedings cold is to declare that she feels alienated by what is going on. At its worst, overprocessing leads to long, exhausting meetings. One group reports that its weekly business meeting of three hours has stretched into eight in the effort to hear everyone out. Small wonder that burnout is a common complaint! Sometimes a whole group will retreat into process in order to avoid a difficult decision. There seems to be a sort of Parkinson's law: the time spent on any agenda item is in inverse proportion to its long-term importance. At its best, the encouragement to each person to voice her feelings and opinions leads to new insights and more creative decisions. Striving toward this goal, one group writes: "We are consciously trying to develop ways of maximizing our productivity without subverting the process"; and another has adopted as a rule of thumb, "Don't get personal unless it helps to get the work done."

Among the structures and procedures that women's groups are using to express feminist values and to enable a group to work together effectively on a task are the following:

1. *Open agendas*, to which everyone is invited to contribute. Sometimes a group will construct and prioritize the agenda as a way of beginning the meeting; sometimes items are turned in ahead of time to an agenda committee.

2. *Rotate tasks.* This procedure allows as many as possible to experience the responsibilities of power; it allows individuals to acquire new skills; it reduces the dependence of the group on a single individual. It is important to rotate tasks often enough so that they do not become the exclusive property of one person; however, the individual should remain in a task long enough to learn to handle it well. Many groups routinely rotate the tasks of the presider or facilitator of the meetings, as well as the recorder. This not only prevents undue concentration of power in the hands of a few, but allows the facilitator and recorder of the previous meeting to participate fully in the next one.

3. *Rotate the representative role* (cf. discussion on page 70).

63

4. *Distribute routine tasks as equally as possible.*

5. *Agree on ground rules for communication* (e.g., speaking from the "I," sharing feelings, giving feedback constructively, and so on).

6. *Stress accurate reporting and open decision-making in the handling of finances.*

7. *Encourage individuals to develop new skills,* not only through job rotation but through apprenticeships and other opportunities for training. The opportunity for growth and development of skills is one of the main incentives feminist groups can offer their members.

8. *Diffuse information frequently to all members.* Knowledge is power. When an informal network monopolizes new information, they can easily become a power block.

9. *Allocate tasks according to criteria of ability, interest, and responsibility rather than popularity.* It is important to recognize and reward existing skills as valuable group resources, and to provide opportunities for those who do not have these skills to learn them.

10. *Develop procedures for sorting out priorities and testing for consensus.* Groups have learned not to assume that silence means consent when testing for consensus. They have developed methods for stating alternatives clearly and specifically enough to make real prioritizing possible.

11. *Assign tasks to a team of two people.* NOW has used this method of sharing responsibility successfully in many of its functions.

12. *Make use of a task force structure that disbands once the task is completed,* thus preventing a concentration of power and increasing organizational flexibility. The Center for Women and Religion has made frequent use of this structure under the title of "Disappearing Task Force."

13. *Develop appropriate structures as the group grows larger and tasks become more complex.* Some groups handle the diversity of tasks by setting up specialized project committees, which, in turn, are integrated through a steering

committee and through a periodic open meeting for policy-making.

The purpose of all this is not to claim these procedures as feminist inventions, but simply to note that after the first flush of enthusiasm for leaderless groups and spontaneity, women's groups have been adopting and adapting explicit structures and procedures as carriers of their values.

Women's Socialization as Influencing Alternative Structures

In the midst of the struggle to form alternative structures, it may be useful to look at the ways in which women have been socialized in American society. Before she ever arrives, every woman in any of our organizations has internalized parts of several more or less conflicting modes of socialization.

In the patriarchal family structures, women learn a kinship modality: learning how to make, or allowing to be made; to behave as daughters, sisters, wives, mothers. These roles are conceived as supportive, nurturant, complementary to the main—i.e., paternal—role. The underlying concept is one of superior and subordinate. In the patriarchal educational system and in other businesses women learn to internalize the mutually exclusive complement to this first socialization: learn how to be one of the boys, to compete for a main rather than a supporting role. The choice for a woman is to become either a mother or a "pater." In its most extreme form, the woman who has made it becomes a patriarch vis-à-vis other women in the system.

In the women's liberation movement, women learn what might be called a class modality, not in the sense of social class—since women are found in all social classes—but rather in the sense of a social caste. (Cf. Helen Hacker, Mary Daly, and others who have analyzed the sex role

65

stratification in our culture as constituting a caste system.) The feminist critique of the oppression of women has as its other side the call to sisterhood; that is, solidarity among women across divisions of race and social class. Feminists see themselves both as peers to the "pater" and as sisters to other women.

Most literature about conflicting socializations for women discusses the conflict within the patriarchal modalities: daughter, sister, wife, mother vs. one of the "paters." The literature does not discuss the conflict for feminists between the patriarchal modality and the feminist alternative. Women often find themselves caught between the dominant/subordinate, vertical, product-oriented relationships that characterize patriarchal life and the feminist alternative, with its emphasis on lateral bonding, process orientation, and peer relationships.

These conflicting patterns of socialization significantly affect the internal workings of women's organizations and efforts for institutional change. Greater awareness of the effects of socialization upon attitudes and on the ways of working and organizing can free women to develop new models. The remainder of this chapter looks at the effects of socialization patterns on work styles, staff models, and board and staff relations. Chapter 5 deals with some of the ways our socialization influences our choice of strategies for institutional change.

Work Styles

Associated with our[3] patriarchal socialization is the conventional product-oriented work style, with its hierarchy of skills, roles, and rewards; a chain of command accountability; and the de-emphasis on personal concerns as irrelevant or secondary. Associated with our feminist socialization is the process-oriented style, with its emphasis on participation, sharing of both responsibilities and chores, collective decision-making, and care for personal concerns. At times we may experience this opposition as an absolute dichotomy, in which case at one end of the spectrum we find the authoritarian director defining the goals, delegating the tasks, and evaluating the results, while riding roughshod over the feelings and needs of other staff members. This pole may get the work done, but it tends to produce marked passivity in the staff: "Just tell us what to do and we'll do it." At the other end we get the collective, dedicated to process and often exhausting the energies of a group in the effort to meet every individual's needs. This pole tends to react against productivity and may even in some situations (e.g., in an educational setting like SQAG) refuse any responsibility for products. It also tends to reinvent the wheel, since group members find it difficult to accept goals or policies that they themselves have not formulated.

However, if we can view the patriarchal and the feminist modes dialectically, as defining the outer limits of a whole repertoire of possible behaviors, we can use the polarity, not as forced choice but as a way to analyze a situation and arrive pragmatically at an appropriate course of action. Just as a wholistic approach seeks to integrate the polarities of thought and feeling, theory and practice, so it must seek to integrate product and process. Surely, any group that wishes to exist and function with some satisfaction to its members and some effect on its environment must deal with both task and maintenance functions, must affirm both the fundamental equality of its members and the differences they bring to the common life and work.

Let us turn to some key elements of the internal structures of women's groups and analyze them in the light of the polarity between the two modes of socialization.

Staff Models

Most of the programs we examined used a variety of

staffing patterns: full-time and part-time, paid staff on minimum wage and on professional salary, and volunteers. This variegated population brings to the staff different (and unequal) skills and experiences; unequal longevity on the job; diverse expectations, colored by different socializations; moreover, staff work unequal hours for unequal pay (anything from a professional salary to the legal minimum for a work-study student to no pay for volunteers). Typically, there is a paid staff member called either the director or the coordinator, but whichever word is used, the other is implicit, together with the underlying ambivalence about leadership roles and styles. Attracted by the feminist character of the programs, the women inside our organizations expect a lateral bonding within the group, a collective style of work, a sisterhood of peers who will be genuinely concerned for one another. They may also expect that working in an all-women group will be a kind of nirvana.

The unanalyzed expectations that everyone brings to the situation quite often result in the highest expectations of both systems being placed on the highest paid staff. Here is the way one director describes her experience:

> I am an authority figure; they expect me to be authoritative and when I am, I am called on it; when I am not, I am called on it. Each person on the student staff expects personal support and friendship as well as instant supervision at her convenience. "You wouldn't have so many problems if you could learn to say no, but not to me." I am expected to be available for three hours of personal counseling, or to have ideas about the newsletter, and also to get all the regular work done as usual.

Another example: The director may be expected to do all her own typing and also to perform all the representative functions outside the organization, functions that usually figure prominently in her job description. Often all this is supposed to be done on a half-time schedule! Perhaps the polarities can be used here to demonstrate the contradiction in the expectations and to reduce the job description to manageable proportions. If the organization is putting a high priority on educating people through the work process, then it must reduce its demands for productivity, or vice versa. Either priority can be legitimate, depending upon the organization's concrete situation; what matters is to be clear about the priorities and to frame the staff roles realistically in relation to them.

The representative role brings it own set of problems. It has often been pointed out that even in traditional hierarchies the representative is a "boundary person," interpreting the organization to the institution and vice versa. In this role, she/he often becomes distrusted by both groups and is the object of hostile projections by both. These difficulties are apt to increase when the representative is communicating on behalf of a feminist collective to a traditional hierarchical group via their director, the situation in which all women's organizations in theological education find themselves. Even rotation of the representative will not solve the problem, since outside groups tend to assume that whomever they communicate with *is* the director and to interpret her actions accordingly, no matter what she says.

For the director/coordinator still another factor makes for isolation. She has no colleagues within the de facto hierarchy and none outside, since most of these women's organizations are one of a kind in their institutions. Lacking a real collegial body, committed for a similar period of time, with similar responsibilities, she colludes with the rest of the staff in setting up a false collectivity; false because it ignores the very real differences in role, time commitments, and rewards among staff members.

But if the highest paid staff experience the highest expectations and the most contradictory demands, the less well paid experience their own share of contradictions and difficulties, not least of which is poor pay. As work-study students, clerical staff, or volunteers, they may perform many of the same functions as directors/coordinators, at a fraction of the salary or none at all. Ironically, it is often the case that the greater the effort to work collectively, rotate tasks, and share decision-making, the more such inequities increase. Consistent with the idealized collective mode, students may have been hired under false pretenses (or at least not disabused of their unrealistic expectations); for example, expecting a job in a collective and finding that they have to work in a conventional mode after all. Jobs may be ill-defined or not defined at all, with the assumption that staff will design their own; but as they begin to work, they may find that the longer-term staff and director point out the implicit parameters they have unwittingly overstepped. Thus, they learn of their, after all, quite conventional job descriptions by violating them.

In addition, staff may expect the direction and, for a job well done, the rewards of a hierarchical system, neither of which they get; or the self-determination and equal say in policy matters of the feminist mode, which are not really available to them either.

Born of the ensuing frustration, the dynamic of "kill the leader" or the "set you up/shoot you down" reaction occurs: the "set you up" as authority is underpinned by the assumption that there is a leader; and the "shoot you down" as authority is rendered much easier than in a conventional structure because of the intimacy and peer-bonding assumed from the feminist mode and the associated disappearance of sex difference, distance, and mystification that bolster other hierarchies.

Boards, Steering Committees, Advisory Groups

Feminist organizations have experimented with a variety of forms of governance and policy oversight. In the organizations we have looked at, a wide range is represented. The Center for Women and Religion (CWR) has a steering committee, which is largely self-perpetuating—a vestige of its early independence from the control of any other institution. The Women's Theological Coalition (WTC) Women's Committee, a student-dominated group composed of representatives of the Boston Theological Institute (BTI) schools, is embedded in the larger BTI structure. Its formal power is to *propose* policy to BTI, although in fact it manages many aspects of day-to-day life in WTC and makes some key decisions. The Research/Resource Associates Program at Harvard is under the oversight of a committee that includes students. The Training Women for Ministry (TWFM) program is overseen by a steering committee of students from the course, ministry team members (the course instructors), Andover Newton faculty, and denominational and WTC representatives. (This varied group deals with all aspects of the course's life—educational decisions; organizational hassles; hiring ministry team members; evaluating the course's structures, requirements, and achievements; and funding.) And Seminary Quarter at Grailville (SQAG) has an advisory committee composed of past participants, and staff and representatives of Grailville, United Theological Seminary of Dayton, the Commission on Women in Ministry (COWIM), seminary faculties, and participating denominations. It is a self-perpetuating group except for the SQAG participants and staff, who are chosen by their peers.

In some ways the experience of these groups with the bodies to which they are accountable is much the same as the general experience of all nonprofit organizations. For instance, "working boards" have been found to have both advantages and disadvantages. The Women's Committee of the WTC, in addition to its responsibilities for oversight of staff activities, has its own programming function.

71

Committee members, who are mostly students, plan and organize lecture presentations, conferences, workshops, and social events for women in the BTI. They also allocate money from the committee's budget for other groups (mostly women's caucuses in the BTI schools) to mount these kinds of activities. The obvious advantage of a governing committee having this kind of "hand-on" experience is that its members are deeply involved and knowledgeable, especially in the area of their involvement (in this case, program). It is unlikely, therefore, that the Women's Committee would set unrealistically ambitious goals for program. They have had the experience of trying to make things happen, and they know the limits. The disadvantage of the arrangement is that the committee is remote from many other aspects of the coalition's life—managing foundation grants, relations with school administrations, long-range planning and setting of priorities, developing overall strategies to focus the consultative and lobbying work of the staff, and so on. These tasks fall to the professional staff member, the director, and she carries them out largely unsupervised and unaccountable, mostly because the committee is so deeply involved in implementing its annual program of educational events. The director is left to settle for herself which long-term research projects to undertake, how much time to spend on faculty development, how much to pressure a given school. Except for a rare planning session in which both the committee and the director have time to describe in detail what they are doing, there is little opportunity for setting priorities. Both are absorbed most of the time in day-to-day activities that run alongside one another but are not often looked at in relation to one another. The "large picture" is obscured by its many details.

The CWR Steering Committee of fifteen members (three of whom are to be named by boards of the Graduate Theological Union, with the other twelve being self-perpetuating) takes the large picture as its mandate. It tries to exercise overview and make some contribution in all aspects of CWR's work. The advantage of this role for the board is that staff have a source of advice and point of accountability for all their activities. The difficulty arises in the size of the task ("We've taken on an agenda that is much too big"), and in the fact that both board and staff are concerned with the same issues without having delineated clearly their different functions in relation to these issues. "Therefore, there is *always* a question of who should make the decision." Boards with too much to do tend to rubber-stamp staff initiatives, because they are not familiar enough with substantive or organizational issues to raise questions or suggest alternatives; and because they have not sufficiently limited the scope of their work, they become dependent on staff to steer them through overlong agendas.

As we noted before, these problems are by no means unique to feminist organizations. However, at least one issue in the relations between boards and staffs of the organizations we observed does seem to originate in principles and practices of the women's movement. Most of these "boards" include many representatives of (or are dominated by) the constituency the organization intends to serve. This practice (shared by the organizations of other community-conscious movements) runs counter to the trustee tradition in American benevolent undertakings. According to this tradition, most trustees are representatives of the public and are expected to combine with their commitment to the cause a detachment or enlightened disinterest that will balance the effects of deep personal investment (and possibly self-interest) on the part of paid staff. An argument is frequently made from the feminist perspective that "wisdom" is more often grounded in consciously appropriating one's experience rather than in detachment from it. "Boards" of feminist organizations reflect this conviction. They include both paid staff (sometimes all paid staff) and almost invariably a good-sized contingent of "consumers."

On the whole there is satisfaction with the effects of organizing boards on a constituency base. There have been difficulties, of course. The prime one is the almost built-in confusion of the staff role and the board role when members of boards and staffs resemble one another so closely in interests, commitment, and level of investment in the organization. But the rewards are considerable. With the role confusion, many issues are raised: What is a professional? What is the role of salary and of different salary levels? Which kinds of status differences are helpful and which are harmful? What rights do "consumers" have? What rights do "providers" (staff) have? These are key issues for women at work, and most of us have found it satisfying to deal with them in board-staff dialogue, as we do our work of advocacy for women.

We return to the question with which this section began: How can we organize ourselves to work effectively as a collective without hierarchy but not without structure? Our struggle is rendered much more difficult by our socialization and the unresolved resentments it has left in its wake: reaction against structure, ambivalence about power, distrust of leadership, distrust of other women. In programs like SQAG and TWFM, where there is a minimum of external structure and a real "free space" in which women can construct their own tasks and ways of working, it takes a long time for the participants to work through their counterdependency and overreaction to the point where they can face the problems inherent in any human cooperation.

Tasks of any complexity require role differentiation and delegation of responsibility. Role differentiation in turn requires careful reintegration of the differences (e.g., through free-flowing communication, shared policy-making and priority setting) if a group is to maintain its cohesion. The problem is compounded for women's groups by the range of diversities—race, social class, life-styles—they are striving to encompass. How much diversity can be integrated into a collective mode? In what respects must the members of a collective be equal for it to be a true collective? Must there be equal commitment, equal time spent on the job, equal rewards, equal decision-making power? Some diversities seem inevitable: long-term and short-term, more or less talented, more or less formally educated; some have been deliberately chosen out of the feminist concern for inclusiveness: race, class, life-style; some seem to result more from inadequate budgets: volunteers, work-study students, part-timers. How can we integrate these differences without developing resentments that ultimately splinter the group? Must we accept limits to the diversity we can encompass? If so, what are these limits?

From the above discussions it is clear that alternative spaces are not nirvana, nor by attempting to construct them do we escape from such limitations of the human condition as imperfect communication, personal jealousies, and unmet needs.

The way to a workable collective style is booby-trapped with false expectations, and demands a high level of discernment and great self-discipline. Discernment is necessary to recognize which limitations come simply from working in a group and striving to accomplish a task, and those which arise from inappropriate or contradictory patterns of socialization. It is difficult to separate an authentic feminist vision from the unrealistic expectations of ideal relationships that "women's collective" conjures up for many women. The collective style—like the Quaker meeting use of consensus decision-making—requires self-restraint on the part of all participants. We need to be able to distinguish self-development from self-absorption in ourselves and to curb our own needs for attention and domination, our own defensiveness and negativism. We need to accept the difficult discipline of helping one another to move away from these destructive behaviors, being open to listen to criticism without defensiveness, and taking the responsibility for calling others on their behavior in ways that give support for change rather than induce guilt.

What makes this long, painful struggle worthwhile? First of all, there is the concrete experience of seeing individual women change from passive conformists, doing as they are told while reserving the right to complain, to responsible adults able to take initiative, make decisions, and take responsibility for the results. This experience seems particularly strong in SQAG and in TWFM, both of which use a self-directed learning model. The initial weeks are a painful struggle with unaccustomed tasks—taking responsibility for one's own learning, being accountable to a group of one's peers, forging a workable collective style—but at some point of the process, individuals begin to take hold, to change behavior, and to discover hitherto untapped potentialities in themselves.

Programs that utilize self-directed learning encourage initiative and teamwork among a group of peers able to give one another critical support and supportive criticism. When teamwork is good it is a source of tremendous synergy: the whole is greater than the sum of its parts.

There is also the openness for experiment, the willingness to try new ways of realizing shared values. And finally, there is the sense of creating a new reality by living new relationships. At least briefly and intermittently, we experience ourselves as peers sharing our gifts and know that the dream of a society where there is neither top dog nor underdog can become a reality, because already we have lived it.

CHAPTER 5

Power and Institutional Change

It is a feminist truism that the personal is political; that is, the oppressions women experience in their daily lives stem from societal structures. Hence, it follows that individual changes—whether in attitudes, values, or behavior; whether brought about by consciousness-raising, education, therapy, or conversion—touch only one aspect of the problem. In fact, a strategy that concentrates solely on changing individuals is something of a two-edged sword. It tends to reinforce the assumption that women are somehow deficient and in need of remedial programs to bring them up to standard; and it furnishes the system with a handy excuse for not making any changes. This is not to deny the real benefits in increased insight, self-esteem, skill development, and support networks that large numbers of women have received through consciouness-raising and other groups, but only to insist that systemic evils demand systemic changes.

Feminists have made great strides in dealing with the personal obstacles to change—the sexist attitudes which have been internalized—but women are still at the beginning in attacking the oppressive structures that institutionalize sexual inequalities. Moreover, sexism does not stand alone; it is intimately connected with racism, classism, imperialism; it supports and is supported by economic, political, legal, and social systems and is sanctioned by religious institutions. Once women begin to

77

grasp the ways in which these systems interlock, it becomes clear that structural change is essential and that it will necessitate dealing with power and power structures.

In the case of women in theological education, the existing programs, despite all their limitations, have served to raise consciousness and to empower individuals to take the risks of action. The painful and frustrating gap between the vision of what could be and the day-to-day experience of what is generates the energies to push for change. These attempts inevitably involve women in the politics of power and in the multiple, and often contradictory, forces for and against institutional change. These experiences have shed new light on feminist understandings of power and on the development of strategies and tactics for institutional change.

Women and Power

Most of the women in our programs are white and have access to economic resources. We will deal first with their experience of power and powerlessness, and then with the experience of racial minority women and women who have been forced to deal with basic economic survival issues, recognizing that generalizations which may hold true for one of these groups do not necessarily hold true for the others.

As white women in theological education, we have experienced power chiefly as something that can be given or denied to us by others. When we endeavor consciously to name our experience, we speak of power as "oppressive," "hierarchical," "destructive." We see power as "power over," as coercion and therefore sin. One who reads the history of our programs can see the disproportionate amounts of energy—the endless planning, strategizing, and struggling—expended simply in getting out from under the power of those who are determining our lives in

78

the institutional setting. We are denied equal access to available resources; we are told what we need and what our questions should be. We do not have the power to determine our own environment—its symbols, myths, and support structures. Often we must expend so much energy in struggling to obtain our own space that we have little energy left for creative work within it. Those of us who were hired as associates in the R/RA at Harvard frequently felt ourselves caught in an endless cycle of preparing reports, organizing and speaking in defense of our program, writing proposals and budgets to keep it going for one more year, only to find it was time to begin the process all over again for the next year. We were dependent on the good will and charity of the group in power. Little wonder, then, that many women in our programs react negatively to the concept of power, insisting either that "we don't have any power" or "we don't want any power," since in our experience having power is equivalent to being oppressors.

But there are many dimensions to the power issue, and often women are ambivalent about it. The tendency is to view power as a masculine sin, a socialization that drives men to keep women in their places, and that expresses itself at the personal level in rape and at the societal level in war. But power is also recognized as a masculine virtue, a strength that in women's fantasy lives furnishes a dream of male protection and care.

Women in our culture, and particularly women in the Christian tradition, have been socialized to be good and kind, to refuse to use power, to regard it as unfeminine and unchristian. For most white women it has been hard to distinguish between assertiveness and aggressiveness. Not accustomed to think of themselves as strong or powerful, nor as persons who have rights, including "a perfect right" to stand up for themselves, women have been brought up to put the needs of others (husband, children, parents) before their own, to yield for the sake of peace, and to regard any

79

other behavior as "selfish." Women tend to lump together the overpowering behavior that tramples the rights of others and the assertive behavior that refuses to be trampled on and to label both as "aggressive." It takes careful analysis to clarify the concept of assertion as the rightful affirmation of personal needs in the face of opposition.

It is a mistake to envision power as a fixed quantity in a given situation, a concept of something static, a thing which can be passed from hand to hand, so that if one has it, another cannot. A more authentic concept is to understand power dynamically as a vital process of empowerment. Then it is clear that it is not a fixed quantity, but can increase or decrease as the persons involved see different possibilities in a situation and move to actualize them.

A good many feminists have seized upon this concept of empowerment as relevant to their experience and more congenial than the usual concepts of power. To be empowered is to experience the value of oneself, to take the self seriously in the totality of one's reality—body, mind, history, vision, and dreams. To be empowered is to feel oneself expanding, getting in touch with one's own needs and goals, developing powers of decision, acquiring new skills, becoming able to do things formerly feared or viewed as impossible.

As valuable as this process of empowerment has been, it has tended to keep us from coming to terms with the realities of our own power and powerlessness and our use of power. Many feminists have tried to distinguish sharply between empowerment as development of one's own strength, and power as "power over" another. Thus, women have separated "personal power" and "social power," approving the former as "control over my own life" and disowning the latter as "control over others." But the case is not so simple. Modestly, I may claim only the right to control my own decisions without wishing to control others, recognizing, of course, that the other has the same rights as the self. But my needs conflict with the real needs of others; human beings are interdependent. If I want wholesome food to eat, clean air to breathe, pure water to drink, to say nothing of adequate health care, a living wage, an end to racial discrimination, I need social power; that is, a real voice in the allocation of resources and services, which in turn involves a measure of control over others. This returns women to the question of how to behave when rightful self-affirmation meets resistance.

In the analysis of our programs we have discovered that we generally respond to the power issue in one of three main ways (or some combination of them). As white middle-class women in a racist and classist society, we have become aware of our privileges: we are well nourished, well educated, enjoy easy access as Americans to resources that are pitifully scarce in much of the rest of the world. We become aware of ourselves as privileged but powerless. Often our first response to this recognition has been guilt, followed by denial. We resent the recognition of our privileges and often try to give them up, an attempt that puts us in the position of trying to deny much of what we are—our backgrounds, families, resources, personalities, gifts. Both guilt and denial reinforce the experience of ourselves as powerless and tend to trap us into immobility. If we do not acknowledge the power we possess, how can we use it? Attempts to organize and strategize appear as either impossible or manipulative. Attempts to give power may alleviate guilt, at least for a time, but they also diminish responsibility and lead to immobilization.

A second way we deal with our power is to try to equalize it, to structure our lives and our groups to provide equal access to all avenues of power. The struggle to equalize power has been a source of some of our greatest learnings and our greatest pain. Chapter 4 examined some of the structures we have devised, as we learn through our individual and collective histories to share, to trust, to assert ourselves, and to affirm one another. As we have begun to sort out the differences between carrying out particular functions and playing a meaningful part in decision-making, we have been able to build more workable structures.

A third approach to power is to seek and demand accountability. We acknowledge our power, we want to use it well, and we are willing to be accountable for its use. This approach assumes that some aspects of our power are not interchangeable—skin color, for instance, or special gifts give us different access to power no matter how much we equalize our internal structures. But if we see power not as a fixed quantity, but as an increasing possibility for those who claim it, we can use the differences to increase the power in a group. Once we recognize that given conditions do not necessarily determine us, we can begin to develop new sources of power. Most of our program ideas arose in situations where the accepted power patterns completely bypassed us. We developed new sources of funding; we learned to get things done without funding; we discovered the power of "inappropriate" behavior and the strength of collective action. The key factor in this approach is the development of accountability structures that enable us to have access to one another's gifts and creativity. Power, then, becomes expansive rather than destructive. To make demands, to confront, to give up or share power become tasks of consciousness-raising and creativity. We learn to recognize and to develop power; we learn to use it and not let ourselves or others use power over us or against us.

The experience of the racial minority women in the programs examined here provides a broader understanding of the potential and the misuse of power.

The black women have spoken of a sense of living in double or triple jeopardy. One writes: "If we are willing to grasp the factual realities of oppressed people, we will discover not only the pervasive influence of the 'rightness of whiteness,' but we will also see clear-cut evidence of the so-called 'rightness of maleness,' and the 'rightness of the haves over against the have-nots.' We live daily in a triple bind—being poor, black, and female in this society." The black women have a clear sense of fighting for justice for blacks. The issues are survival issues, and most black women seminarians have much closer ties to the black community and the black churches than to the seminaries. The white institutions have never been a source of power for them, and therefore their sense of self is not tied to the institution as it is for many white women.

Out of the context of double and triple jeopardy, many black women have developed a strong sense of the need for survival. They expect things to be taken away and are always prepared for loss. Repeatedly, they have had the experience of hitting bottom and have had to begin the long climb once again. Consequently, they have a kind of sustaining power, an ability to persevere through difficulties that has sometimes been lacking in white women's groups. Many white women have been brought up to fear failure and have no conviction that they can survive through failures; as a result, they may lack staying power for a sustained struggle. Our discussions illuminated other differences, flowing from the fact that white middle-class women have not had to deal with survival issues. "I assume survival," writes a Southern white woman. "Much of what I wanted and needed has come to me, often without my asking. I never learned to calculate, because I could get by without doing that . . . others would take care of me . . . I could sit back and let the world go by." Thus, some white women tend to approach organizational work without a clear agenda of their own and to drift through committee meetings. On the contrary, black women tend to be highly goal-oriented, focused on the outcomes they want to bring about and ready to plan and act strategically.

Many black women have found a sense of identity and a

source of affirmation in their churches, despite the "rightness of maleness" that may be present in church structures. Often they have a strong sense of call that does not depend upon official recognition. There is a long history of black women preachers and founders of local churches who have been powerful because of what they did, not because they were ordained or officially commissioned. In the black experience, faith, community, and social justice have often been integrated into a source of power that the programs of white women are still struggling to experience.

Wherever individual women may be in terms of dealing with their feelings about power, women's groups and programs find themselves obliged to take action in the institutional power arena.

When we consider the possible courses of action, there appear to be two basic strategies we can use for bringing about institutional change: (1) providing alternative services or institutions and (2) changing existing institutions; that is, changing the decisions of the decision-makers. To illustrate the difference, let us take the issue of helping women to establish credit for taking out loans. A group can provide a service of information and counseling for women on how to go about getting loans; it can set up an alternative institution, such as a women's credit union that will actually make loans, using a somewhat different set of criteria than the banks; or it can change the policies of the existing institutions so that banks and loan companies establish a more just set of criteria for making loans.

Alternative Institutions as Change Strategies

The model of the alternative institution, set up outside the established structures, has a strong appeal to women. All one's energy can go directly into building a model of things as they could and should be; moreover, it would seem, at least at first, that one does not have to deal with questions of power, confrontation, negotiation, and this too is appealing to many women. The women's movement has produced countless examples of alternative services and institutions: Women's Yellow Pages, presses, publications, theater and film-making collectives; credit unions, banks, carpentry collectives, alternative businesses; rape crisis centers, child care centers, shelters for battered women, hot lines; continuing education programs, assertiveness training, women's studies programs; self-help health clinics, therapy collectives, self-defense classes, centers for feminist theologizing.

The alternatives have a number of advantages. On the one hand, the services provide a way of making contact with nonfeminists and spreading ideas; those who staff the programs have opportunities to grow personally, to develop skills, to acquire in-depth knowledge of an area or problem. Not least, the alternative has autonomy; those involved are free to implement their plans without external interference. On the other hand, the alternatives are hard to finance and maintain, and in fact these projects have a high mortality rate. They drain the energies of the staff, and may tend to orient participants toward passively receiving services rather than toward learning to take active control of their own lives. Often they reach only a few people; they may become ingrown—a group which has struggled together to start a new program or project may become so comfortable together that they are unable to integrate new members and, in effect, become a closed community.

Some alternative institutions have been highly creative, but even a strong demonstration that another way is possible may not have much effect on the established institutional structures as such. The establishment can easily ignore the alternative or may even use governmental power to suppress it (e.g., the battle in the courts waged by the medical fraternity against the women's self-help clinics).

In this connection it is instructive to look at the example of the private foundations, which often use a strategy of funding a demonstration project in the hope of producing a multiplier effect. Even though they wield the power levers of funding and prestige, and generally are not promoting particularly radical changes, they experience difficulty in getting a new program adopted by the mainline institutions. As the experience of CWR and TWFM has shown, unless an institutional commitment to continue the program is built into the original grant as a requirement, the institution may reap the benefits while the grant lasts and then eliminate the program. If the alternate makes real inroads on the clientele of the institution, the institution may adopt some of the features of the innovation. Thus, in the 60s the universities, under pressure from the student movement and the free universities, set up offices for innovative education, provided pass/fail grading options, individualized degree programs, and the like; similarly, under pressure from the women's movement, they have inaugurated women's studies courses and degree programs.

Another danger for the alternate is encapsulation: those on the outside may label it in a way that enables them to dismiss the issue. They may say, "Let those 'radicals,' 'hippies,' 'gays,' do their thing over there in their own space; it's no concern of ours." When this happens the separated space results in blunting the issue rather than sharpening it. In short, the mere existence of an alternate does not appear to constitute an action strategy; the alternate needs to become part of a broader plan that actively engages the institution.

Changing the Decisions of the Decision-makers

If the alternate opts for linkage with the institution, several questions arise: How closely to tie into the existing structures? How to divide energies between building up one's own space and attempting to influence the larger system? Do we want to be "at" or "of" the larger system? lightly linked or definitely part of? How will we get our funding? Do we want to be totally dependent on the larger system or to seek some independent source of funds? How far can we go in challenging the system if we are dependent on it for funding? Autonomy and financial security would seem to be in inverse relation to each other.

The programs in our sample range from SQAG, which was set up and funded outside the seminary system (except for its linkage with United Theological Seminary for handling student credit hours), to TWFM and the R/RA, which are formally part of the institutions, albeit on a less-than-permanent basis.

Once a group has become part of a larger system and is committed to bringing about changes in that system, it has a range of possible strategies, from cooperative to confrontative, that it can use in its attempts to change the decisions of the decision-makers.

1. *Using regular channels:* proposals to the appropriate committee for new appointments, regulations, or procedures; the appointment of a woman to the faculty; the approval of a women's studies course. The greater the change, the more internal politicking will probably be involved: discreet conversations with key members of the decisive committee, soliciting expressions of support from influential members of the community, and other lobbying tactics. These methods are usually slow and cumbersome, and can be expected to yield only incremental gains.

2. *Organizational development:* using a combination of outside and inside consultants, workshops on team-building and problem-solving, and similar educational strategies to improve communication, change individual attitudes and behaviors, and introduce new ideas into the system. Outside consultants are often helpful, since they can give

87

feedback to the members of any organization more freely and objectively than those within the system.

3. *Data feedback:* using questionnaires or similar data-collecting devices to gather information about the system and then feeding back the results. Data feedback is often able to tell members of an organization things they did not know about their collective life. The strategy here is to demonstrate the discrepancy between the stated goals of the organization and its actual operations. One example of this technique is the Council on Women and the Church (COWAC) survey of the seven United Presbyterian seminaries in this country. By means of questionnaires, followed up by interviews with the seminary administrators, this committee carefully assembled data on the large percentage of women students and the miniscule proportion of women faculty, administrators, and trustees in each seminary. It pointed up the discrepancies between the statistics and the formal policy statement of the church and made a series of highly specific recommendations. Similarly, the YWCA, in its 1971 institutional racism audit, used a questionnaire to gather data about the differential between blacks and whites in access to resources and participation in decision-making within each institution studied. This method works particularly well with religious organizations, which are often vulnerable to a vigorous critique in terms of their own stated goals. Ultimately, data feedback makes a direct appeal to the conscience of the decision-makers and depends on their openness and good will for its effectiveness. The rhetoric is one of playing on the liberal commitment (and the guilt) of the institution and can make good use of the language of reparations: women's issues are a question of justice and not just of institutional beneficence.

4. *Going by the book:* a standard technique wherever the organization has a book of rules or standard procedures. Insisting on obeying the letter of the law may throw the

88

system into such confusion that a demand will be met. This strategy may be useful in pressing for scholarship grants or in dealing with discrimination in examinations for ordination.

5. *Building an internal power base:* by identifying supportive individuals within the system (a dean, a department chairperson, a denominational leader, a member of the board of trustees, a professor, a student leader) and then orchestrating their efforts to secure a given result. This may be done quietly by one or two women advocates working in the background. Thus, in one seminary, over a five-year period, a woman administrator working with a few female students to build a power base was able to increase the number of women students from 35 to 135 and the women faculty from 0 to 6. Or it may be done in the spotlight, with a set of explicit demands, a model some of the women's caucuses in the churches, seminaries, and learned societies have used to good effect.

6. *Forming coalitions with groups outside the institution:* On the seminary scene, coalitions between faculty women and churchwomen have been particularly fruitful. Often churchwomen have access to independent sources of funds or are in a position to pressure the church structures for funds, and are willing to use these resources in support of women in ministry. Thus, TWFM was established because of close collaboration between an Andover Newton faculty member, the WCT of the Boston Theological Institute (BTI), and the United Church of Christ Task Force on Women in Church and Society, which had access to the necessary funding and was committed to developing professional church leadership among women.

7. *Using federal affirmative action legislation to pressure the institution:* Thus, the Women's Equity Action League (WEAL) has brought class-action suits against a number of universities, charging sex discrimination. The question of whether any of this legislation can be applied to seminaries

is complex, and any group planning to use it will need the assistance of a lawyer well versed in the intricacies of Executive Order #11246 and Titles 6, 7, and 9. The strongest provisions forbidding discrimination based on sex in recruiting, hiring, and promotion apply only to federal contractors and invoke the loss of such contracts as the ultimate means of securing compliance. However, most seminaries do not qualify as federal contractors, even though they may receive federal work-study funds for their students. Brigham Young University has brought a test case to establish the point that handling work-study funds does not make the institution a federal contractor within the meaning of the law. It is not entirely clear whether a divinity school which is part of a university that is definitely a federal contractor (by virtue of receiving federal research grants, funds for library improvement or for construction) thereby falls under the strongest affirmative action legislation. Educational institutions that are controlled by a religious organization (which is the case of most seminaries) are specifically exempt if the application of the act would be inconsistent with the religious tenets of the organization. Title 9, which is clearly against any form of discrimination based on sex, does not provide a remedy beyond a letter of findings and its attendant publicity. Since much of this legislation is quite new, the Office of Federal Contract Compliance is interested in test cases and can be approached for support by a group interested in bringing suit. Even the possibility of an affirmative action suit, together with the unfavorable publicity such a suit could generate, may be enough to exert some pressure for change on the institution.

8. *Seizing power and confronting the administration:* as the student movements of the 60s did. Perhaps seizing is too strong a word; taking an unexpected initiative might be a more accurate way of describing the more confrontative end of this spectrum of tactics. As discussed above, power is

not a fixed quantity in any situation; there are always untapped potentialities in the people involved, unexplored alternatives for action—what Saul Alinsky called "the positive in the negative." If the leadership is able to formulate such an initiative, it almost always releases energies in the group, energies that tend to build under the stimulus of action. Initiative from an unexpected quarter is experienced as a threat by the establishment, which characteristically overreacts. An alert group will capitalize on the overreaction to win concessions from the powers that be. A variety of tactics are available within this category:

—*Demonstrating strength in meetings with the authorities.* This technique is especially effective when it takes the authority by surprise. For example, in the initial stages of negotiating for a women's center on one seminary campus, the two group leaders came to their appointment with the dean accompanied by twenty-five other women and a tape recorder, thus serving notice to the dean that he would be held accountable for his promises.

—*Redefining the issues from within the system.* The Catholic Women's Ordination Conference headlined the brochure announcing its second conference with the challenge, "It is time to lay to rest the heresy that women cannot image Jesus in the priesthood," and defines itself as "working to create a new Church and a new priestly ministry."

—*Publishing "with intent to maim or kill,"* giving local or national exposure to sexist practices and policies, as the CWR staff did in an instance of discrimination in hiring that violated the school's own practices and procedures. Publicizing such a case embarrasses the authorities and may help to rouse public opinion and either generate pressures for change or at least serve as a deterrent to repetition (as in the case of the judge who was forced to resign in the furor which followed his remark that it was "normal" for a sixteen-year-old boy to rape an attractive young girl). Sometimes the threat of publicity is a sufficient deterrent. Sexual harassment is a serious and difficult problem for women not only in business, but in graduate schools and seminaries. One woman has suggested that the individual dealing with this issue hide a small tape recorder on her person as a way of defendng herself and, if need be, securing the removal of the offender from the system.[1]

—*Symbolic acts within the public view,* as when the Berrigan brothers poured blood on draft records as a way of dramatizing the issues of the Vietnam War. Recently, the Catholic Women's Ordination Conference has come forth with "funny money"—oversize, obviously counterfeit bills for the church collection plate which announce that the donor will continue to contribute that sum to the ordination conference until the church changes its policy on the ordination of women. While this device has not yet received wide publicity, it has been effective in raising the issue at the parish level.

—*Civil disobedience,* the deliberate breaking of a law that the lawbreakers regard as unjust. The illegal ordination of the eleven Episcopal women to the priesthood brought about widespread discussion of the issue and succeeded in changing church policy and practice.

—*Disrupting the institution,* whether by one-shot or prolonged, mild or strong-arm tactics. The 60s gave us demonstrations, sit-ins, student strikes, boycotts. The effectiveness of these techniques depends on whether the planners are clear about their goals and have adapted their techniques accordingly. Disruptions are usually successful in gaining publicity and

92

enabling the group to air an issue. They may also be used to build a sufficient power base to force a specific change. Thus, women at one seminary, on an appointed day, wore police whistles to class and literally "blew the whistle" on every use of sexist language, an effective means of achieving a very quick change in language patterns. Student demonstrations have also been effective in securing tenure for controversial professors. Sometimes, however, it is difficult to assess the effectiveness of mass actions: one hundred students walked out of Princeton Theological Seminary in protest without inducing any immediately perceptible change in that institution. Similarly, a group of Glenmary sisters in Cincinnati and a majority of the Immaculate Heart of Mary congregation in Los Angeles resolved lengthy confrontations with their respective bishops by removing themselves from the institutional structures; actions that did not appear to have much immediate effect on diocesan procedures, although they undoubtedly produced strong reverberations and changed consciousness in other quarters.

In analyzing the strategies used by women's programs in theological education, particularly the seven highlighted in this volume, it is clear that, although they used different tactics at different times, their methods cluster at the cooperative end of the scale. What determines the choice of tactics?

The organizational analysts point out that the key factor is the relation of the goals of the two groups to each other. If we achieve our goals, can the others achieve theirs? If so, we are in a win/win situation (e.g., dancing, learning), and a collaborative strategy is indicated—trust-building, open communication, careful checking of perceptions of the other's position, and consistent, predictable behavior. If the answer is no, then we are in a win/lose situation (a poker game, a race, a departmental appointment), and a fight strategy becomes necessary. Fight strategies require building a power base, defining clear and achievable goals, restricting the flow of information (playing one's cards "close to the vest"), bluffing, surprising one's opponents by behavior that is unpredictable and outside their experience, and perhaps personalizing the issue. A fight strategy requires an alertness that takes nothing for granted, and the negotiating skills to drive a hard bargain and pin down the results explicitly, in writing and, if possible, in public. These are skills that women have not had much opportunity to acquire; moreover, many women feel some distaste for these tactics and would prefer to treat all situations as if they were collaborative and appropriate for open and trusting behavior.

In real life there are many situations in which we feel the need to fight and to collaborate simultaneously, situations where we want a more cooperative attitude between the parties but also recognize legitimate areas of conflict. For example, both the seminary and the women's program may want to attract more women students to the school (although for perhaps quite different reasons) but disagree sharply about what resources should be provided when they arrive. Such a situation requires a combination of collaborative and confrontative styles, either in sequence over a period of time or divided between different parts of the group. For example, during the initial period of the WTC, a strong confrontative style was used ("Would anything have started without confrontation at the beginning?"); after the WTC was established as a standing committee of the BTI, with a regular budget, it moved to a collaborative style. In other cases the staff members work collaboratively inside the institution but look to another group—a student lobby, the alumnae, some board members—to use the confrontative tactics. As one staff member remarked, "We need to have the confrontation function carried out, but by somebody else, an outside advocacy group. . . . We have felt confrontation as a severe drawback when we are getting our funding from the same group."

It would seem that the patriarchal socialization of women—at least of white middle-class women—to politeness, suppression of anger, and male dependence also influences the choice of change strategies. It is difficult not to slip into a daughter role with a fatherly dean who is apparently trying to find resources for your program; it is hard to wash the departmental dirty laundry in public and use the ensuing publicity to negotiate for a desired goal when your action causes embarrassment to a friendly colleague. But there are occasions when such strategies are both appropriate and effective. Whether or not it is true that feminists tend to favor confrontational styles, it is certainly useful for all women in theological education to look at both styles. Only by analyzing their advantages and disadvantages is it possible to choose strategies and tactics freely rather than to have them determined by unconscious impulses.

We have already noted that the collaborative mode tends to work within the established structures, while networking or perhaps forming coalitions with groups outside the institution. The advantage of this mode is that the change agents are more likely to be present at inner-circle gatherings (although there are still many barriers for women who seek admittance into the "old boys club") where most key decisions are made. Also, we suspect that the greater the degree of incorporation, the more secure the funding. Those working in the confrontative style risk their access to the inner circle as well as their funding: the patriarchy reacts by cutting off the rebellious daughter's allowance! When developing a confrontative strategy, it is desirable to find some independent sources of funding. The great advantage of this style is that it is easier for the group to maintain its own integrity, sense of purpose, and solidarity with others in the women's movement.

Distinct languages and paradigms characterize each style. In the cooperative style a rhetoric of family relationships is likely to be used; sisterhood is understood primarily in terms of affection, and theological references are apt to be drawn from theologies of reconciliation and healing. The confrontative style tends to use a rhetoric of class politics, speaking of oppressor and oppressed and solidarity; it understands sisterhood primarily in terms of political coalitions, and draws its references from the theologies of liberation.

Each mode has its own dangers. For the collaborative mode the danger is co-optation, being so completely absorbed into the system that your issues are relegated to the bottom of the list or are lost altogether; for the confrontative, the danger is alienation. In either case the organization is marginalized, whether by being totally absorbed or totally ignored. Similarly, the staff may be assimilated back into the system in the one mode or totally alienated in the other. In several instances women hired originally as women's advocates were asked to "lend a hand" in so many other areas that they had little or no time for women's concerns. But a staffer who has engaged in repeated confrontations may become persona non grata to such an extent that she will either be fired or her position will simply not be refunded.

For the individual, it may be difficult to maintain integrity in the cooperative mode. She may feel torn by the contradictions between personal friendships and organizational demand.

Suppose you get into a friendship with one of the power people; he really confides in you, starts telling you his secrets, the unbearable pressures, his private fears. He tells you he is afraid he is going to crack up if he gets one more budget demand. What, if anything, do you tell him about the new budget demands that your women's program is about to make?

Note that there are two levels here. At the organizational level, he expects a *quid pro quo*: "If I tell you my secrets, I expect you to tell me yours: when is your group going to press for funds?" At the personal level, I feel myself living a contradiction that tears me apart: who am I in this network of relationships? Which mode am I operating out of—a friendship, open and trusting mode, or a solidarity/keep my own counsel mode?

In this situation, if the woman operates from the friendship mode, she may forget who her constituency is and what its issues are, the issues which originally drew her into the job. If she remains faithful to the goals and strategy of her group, she may feel she is betraying a friend. The confronter generally does not have the problems arising out of friendship with the establishment; she is more apt to burn out in frustration and rage against the system and the injustice it perpetrates.

Organizations working predominantly in the cooperative mode become hypersensitive to the ebb and flow of events within the institution and therefore need to make special efforts to keep in touch with larger currents. Those strongly linked to regional or national movement groups may become susceptible to every change in the women's movement.

While some groups may be identified more closely with one style than the other, it is obvious that no group restricts itself to one style. Rather, each organization slides along a spectrum, operating out of some combination of collaborative and confrontative styles according to the circumstances prevailing at a particular time.

Advocacy Roles

Advocacy issues afford another illustration of how both collaborative and confrontative styles can work out in

97

practice. What does it mean for women's centers or programs to be advocates for women's concerns? For whom are we acting as advocates? How can advocacy be made more effective?

The question of advocacy arises differently in the various structures of women's programs. Within our sample at least three types of structures are included:

1. The center or program in a single school (R/RA, WCT, TWFM)
2. The organization or center in a consortium (WTC, CWR, BWIM)
3. The alternative model, outside the system (SQAG)

The advocacy role is perhaps clearest for the centers in a single school, for these have the most well-defined constituencies: the women students and the women faculty in that school. They tend to focus their energies on advocating for women's concerns within the institution: additional women's studies courses, additional women on the faculty, more space and resources available for the women students. Advocacy issues have not arisen for SQAG, beyond the basic concern to make an alternative experience available to as many seminary women as possible, a goal around which board members and alumnae have mobilized their efforts.

For the center in a consortium, the question is quite complex. For whom can such a center speak? Who is the constituency? The WTC defines a series of constituencies:

—women students and faculty of the nine BTI schools
—student spouses
—women staff
—women in lay and ordained ministries in the Boston area
—women all over the country asking for information and resources

98

—the national network of persons concerned about women in theological education and the church.

CWR serves a similar constituency, with the addition of Bay Area political groups advocating for women's human rights.

With limited resources and staff, priority-setting is an obvious necessity. How do we balance internal and external advocacy? How much do we want to be (how much are we able to be) involved in regional and national issues?

From the experience of women at the BTI it would seem that a clear decision to take advocacy stands frees a group to use a confrontative style; however, the militant stance is apt to restrict the constituency. When the WTC began to stress the inclusion of diverse feminist perspectives, it greatly increased its constituency but restricted its possibilities for advocacy. On some issues internal to the system, such as the hiring of more women faculty, the increasing of budgets for women's programs by the member schools, there is no problem. The women's coalition is expected to play an advocacy role in these matters. On other issues on which member schools are sharply divided, such as abortion and gay rights, it becomes difficult or impossible for the WTC, as an organ of the consortium, to speak out. CWR, however, has devoted a good deal of energy to playing an advocacy role outside the institution, and has published policy stands on inclusive language and abortion that have been used nationally and internationally.

Centralization or Decentralization

This question is an issue for the consortium centers and for SQAG. Originally, in the consortium schools the women concerned with feminist issues were few in number and scattered over many schools. Centralization was an absolute necessity in order to gather the resources and generate the energies for programming. Initially, the centers concerned themselves with year-to-year programming and, occasionally, with affirmative action faculty hiring. Now, however, as women have entered seminary in increasing numbers, the centers tend to localize in the member institutions: there is a tendency for women's caucuses to form in the BTI schools; similarly, in the Graduate Theological Union, the women students are devoting their major energies to programming within their own schools, surely a healthy development and one that perhaps indicates that time is now ripe for the women's centers to focus on long-range tasks. The CWR suggests the following division of labor:

The centralized agency can effectively do the following:

—Descriptive research about women in ministry: How many are at work in the area? What kinds of work are they doing? What problems do they encounter?
—Faculty development for women's studies programs: Identifying the feminists and parafeminists in the various schools, creating networks among them, then bringing them together in meetings.
—Career education and development: Placement of graduates should be seen as a normal part of the administrative task in the individual schools, except for nationwide services, such as the WTC's Doctoral Placement Service.

Centers in the individual schools should carry the responsibility for year-to-year programming. Each school should develop its own agenda; for example, the women in the Lutheran school are concerned currently with changes in the Lutheran liturgy.

SQAG began as a program at the national level, drawing women from all sections of the country, from a wide variety of religious traditions, and from different types of seminaries: denominational and nondenominational, large and small, prestigious and less well known. One of the strengths of the program has been this diversity and the stimulus and learnings it afforded the participants. The decision to regionalize the program, beginning with a one-week seminar at the Interdenominational Theological Center, in Atlanta, in March of 1977, was made in the hope of reaching out to a larger group of women and increasing the participation of racial minority and low-income women.

Reviewing what various women's groups in theological education have done in their efforts to bring about institutional change, at present it seems perhaps more appropriate to speak of change styles rather than change strategies, for the hand-to-mouth organizational life and the struggle for survival in capricious and unfriendly environments have tended to produce short-range programs of action rather than systematic analyses, well-defined goals, and carefully chosen strategies. As the organizations stabilize and are able to solve the problem of continuity through their boards and long-term staff, they will be able to turn more attention to long-range planning. There is need for a more systematic and sustained analysis to ground the strategies. How conscious are our plans for action? our maps for change? What forces are likely to have determinative influence in changing the churches and seminaries? Contexts like geographical location, the law, theology, and the culture-at-large need to be assessed, so that we can put our energies into maximizing the influences of those contexts most likely to bring about desired changes. How thoroughgoing is our feminist critique of existing concepts of theology as a discipline? of theological education, its structures and practices? Do we have a sufficient analysis of racism and classism to see how these structures interrelate with sexism, and how all three relate to seminary and church structures?

The CWR staff reported that they were charged with

racism for the way in which they organized their consultation on women's studies in theological education in August 1977.

We were charged with racism (in setting up the consultation). We had invited representatives of theological education as we know them. What are the centers of theological education that are not white middle class? As long as we confine ourselves to professional degree programs as defined by the white middle class, we will reflect their racism. We need to bring in other institutions than those already there, other concepts in ministry and preparation for ministry.

Ultimately, we must ask ourselves about the level of change at which we are aiming. We can distinguish four levels:

1. *Changing one element of a system*: getting a new person into an existing job, a woman teaching church history
2. *Changing some small or large part of an existing structure*: introducing team-teaching, establishing a self-directed learning model for a course or set of courses, getting a women's studies course accepted as part of the core curriculum, abolishing tenure
3. *Changing the entire system*: starting a seminary that works directly in churches as a community of co-learners on an action/reflection model
4. *Challenging the premises of the entire social system*: seeking to bring about the revolution that will reconstruct society from its roots, eliminating class, sex, and race privileges in favor of a more humane and liberated world.

Social activists and theorists have debated endlessly the merits of reformist versus revolutionary strategies. As Charlotte Bunch notes in her article "The Reform Tool

Kit," in the women's movement the radicals have tended to be long on analysis and short on programs of action, while the reformist wing has offered a vast array of action programs, involving thousands of women in work for concrete, immediate gains, but has accepted an ideology of equality within the American mainstream.[2] Ideological purity can lead to immobilization before the immensity of the issues; short-term action programs may, in the long run, lead to co-optation unless they are ideologically grounded and regularly evaluated in the light of long-term goals.

The individual woman, deciding whether to put her energies into an establishment institution or an alternative, whether, as SQAG '74 put it, "to be on or off the bus," faces painful contradictions. Marilyn Frye analyzes some of the implications for a woman teaching in a conventional academic structure:

> Sometimes I catch a glimpse of myself in a classroom, in a university building, clothed and fed and insured by the university, before an audience brought there by the university; and I am very seriously spelling out and explaining for them as persuasively as I can a radical feminist perception of the world, and coaching them in the arts of right reason and clear vision so that they will be able to discover for themselves what is going on in this sexist culture. And the better I am at teaching these things . . . the more good I do the institution.
>
> The fact that it allows someone to stand in it and say these things gives it credit in the eyes of the students and the wider public. That I am there saying truths and teaching women makes the whole thing more tolerable for the women. . . . But among the truths is the truth that the institution is male-dominated and directed to serve the ends of a male-dominated society, economy and culture. As such, its existence, not to mention its strength and vigor, is inimical to the welfare of women and probably to the survival of the species. If the women in the class come to agree with me, they must see me then as an absurd figure. For I am just that. . . .

Tokenism is painful, and either resolution of the problem of integration and compromise—joining the boys or becoming a token feminist—immerses the women in the absurdity. For the token feminist, the thing must eventually come down to the question of when, over what issues, and with what provocation, to fight the battle which will lose her her job; or when to reject the absurdity and resign. It is inevitable that it comes to this question. If she is a feminist, her tolerance for sexist abuse must have a limit; if she is unable or unwilling to risk her job, she has no limit; if she can risk it, she eventually will.[3]

How can we be revolutionaries in the context of reform? How can we aim at an ultimate human liberation, deepen our analysis, sharpen our vision, and at the same time continue to act against the oppressions we experience in the concrete circumstances of our daily lives? How can we live with the contradictions and not be rendered immobile or despairing? Beverly Harrison has made the following suggestions:

—We can name the contradictions, not trying to simplify or gloss over or deny them.
—We can take the long view, realizing that significant change does not take place overnight, nor over a decade. The dinosaur moves but slowly. One of the great weaknesses in the ferment of the 60s was the short time span: many young activists expected that a few months or at most a year's work would be crowned with brilliant success and became embittered and cynical when instant results did not materialize.
—Undertake the immediate action, for we do not know which actions will open the door to some more significant changes. As we undertake an action it is of crucial importance to gather together a support group within the institution to help analyze and strategize and build together.
—Be prepared to take the necessary risks. A feminist support group outside the institution is a *sine qua non* for

remaining honest with oneself and avoiding co-optation. Sooner or later, you will have to choose between your principles and your job. To keep the freedom of spirit to make this choice, in addition to your support group you will need some alternative means of economic support.[4]

Ours is a difficult task: to live with the contradictions without either sweeping them under the rug or being immobilized by them, somehow living in hope. Beverly Harrison says, "Hope to me means that knowing what I know, I still get out of bed in the morning, saying, 'I have important things to do today.' It means believing that there is something in our living and dying that isn't lost; that somebody else will be there because we have been there."[5] Feminists who attempt to transform the structures of theological education travel a narrow path between contradictory demands and live with the awareness that they must plunge ahead quickly before more women's lives are damaged by the present system. Such commitment is possible only in a context of hope.

CHAPTER 6

Still Making the Road as We Go

Women's struggle against sexism in theological education has been a striving both to become rooted in hostile soil and to transform that soil's composition. In writing this book, we have stepped back for a moment, pausing to examine that which we have sown. We began with a definition of sexism and with a description of our writing process. These pages are a concrete instance of collective reflection. Through them we have described our struggle against personal, cultural, and institutional sexism and racism in theological education. In reflecting on the various constituencies engaged in women's programs, we have learned that what and how we learn is directly affected by those with whom we study. We described the explicit and implicit racism of our programs and their class bias. We articulated a need for expanding our constituency to provide programming and resources with and for women who are not white and middle class, nor formally educated. We described a model for doing research which demands that our learnings be both intelligible to the nonacademically trained religious person and descriptive of their reality. We have discussed models for staffing programs and for developing nonhierarchical structures.

In our struggle to create new life in old soil, we have confronted sexism as we have experienced it in a lack of power, a lack of access to resources, and a lack of participation in the decision-making structures of institutions of theological education. Reflection on this process has enabled us to clarify various implicit assumptions that link us to the broader feminist movements and to people's movements for liberation. A description of these assumptions, which form the root system of our convictions, follows.

1. *Reflection on our experiences is an essential starting point for learning, for doing theology, for engaging in political activities, and for acting toward systemic change.*

Each chapter explicitly makes a statement about our self-reflection on an experience of self in relation to an aspect of theological education. Our reflections on our individual experiences as women in these settings has led to the articulating of differences and commonalities. This sharing process, in turn, led to an understanding that what appear to be individual and private needs are, in fact, social problems. We then proceeded to the development of strategies rooted in the collective sharing of experiences. In discussing the issue of power, white women describe our experience in a threefold process: (a) the negation/denial of power, (b) empowerment, and (c) the possession and utilization of individual and/or collective power. The experience of black women is different in that our socialization in the individual and the collective realms of theological education and the larger society is one of socialization for survival. Only by reflecting on our respective experiences in the theological context do we understand more fully our differing access to the resources of traditional theological education and our need for/role in creating alternate programs. White women engaged in such sharing have pressed to discover commonalities with black women and to base collaborative action on these commonalities. Black women, however, do not experience commonality as the primary criterion for collaboration. Rather, we understand the need, at times, to risk collaboration that is based not on the experiences of commonalities, but on the importance of the concrete and specific issue. Hence, we have found that in order for black women and white women to work together out of an experiential base, such different perspectives must be clearly articulated and understood by all participants.

2. *The naming and transforming of images and symbols of the spiritual dimensions of our lives is integral to seeking wholeness.*

As women in theological education who have experienced the exclusivity and unacknowledged biases of the white, male, European worldview, we have begun to transform old images and create new symbols of ultimate reality. The initial struggle in theological education and in the churches has been that of combating sexist language and male imagery of the deity in classroom presentations, in liturgy, and in worship. While changes in pronouns, from "him" to "her/him," have occurred, such changes are often token and serve to mask sexist assumptions. Women's criticisms of the misogynist structure of Western language remain unacknowledged.

At its deepest levels, feminist naming and transforming of symbol and image seeks to express that "new reality" in which peoples who have traditionally been excluded and invisible are made central. Through this process the relationship between research, ministry, and spirituality is concretized. Through the creation of new language, new myth, and new symbol we move toward wholeness and begin to undermine present theological structures of exclusivity and oppression.

3. *Shared and collective styles of leadership affirm equality within relationships in organizations and institutions, and can overcome the dominant/subordinate styles of hierarchical leadership.*

In beginning to understand the systemic nature of our exclusion from power and decision-making, we saw the extent to which the hierarchical model of organization was responsible. By being forced into dominant/subordinate roles, those not in power are, by definition, excluded. Hence, in affirming equality within relationships in our organizations, we moved toward shared and collective styles of leadership.

In reflecting on our history of work styles, staffing models, and decision-making, it became clear that collective styles of leadership demand certain structures. We also found that power dynamics, issues of authority, and questions of status do not necessarily disappear within collective models. It has been necessary, therefore, to struggle for new structures and new ways of sharing power and naming our authority. Moreover, the high level of expectations that women have regarding nonhierarchical styles and noncompetitive, woman-led structures further complicates the task of sharing power and decision-making.

As noted in nearly every program description, constituency is a pivotal issue with regard to our assumption about shared leadership. It is a commonly held value but also a potential source for exclusiveness. Power, in terms of access to resources, can be controlled by one subgroup and used destructively. Given the present racial, class, and age composition of women in theological education, we acknowledge the risk of including women from groups currently less well represented, but of maintaining leadership in the hands of the few who created the alternative structure. In this way the constituency of the group may change without necessarily changing the constituency of the leadership. Such an insight has taught us that collective leadership does not guarantee equal participation for all involved and must be understood in relation to the question of constituency.

4. *Equity in access to power and decison-making requires the redistribution of power and new images of power.*

109

In the naming of both our individual and collective experiences, and through the creation of centers, coalitions, and programs, women have claimed their power in theological education. This process has impressed upon us new understandings of empowerment, which have led to the increased sharing of power. We have moved from an experience of our own powerlessness and of the power of men over us to an experience of "power *with*."

Reflections on this process have provided several new insights into our understanding of power. As women within theological education, we find ourselves at odds with one another on the basis of class and race interests. Some white women, after gaining access to resources through group struggle, have tended to divide these resources in benevolent ways with racial minority women. Rather than reflecting a commitment to collectivity, this behavior mirrors the benevolent practices of patriarchal institutions. Women must continue to struggle against the prevailing practices by which limited resources are distributed by those in power according to *their* priorities. We must demand of ourselves and of mainline institutions a redistribution of power and resources in ways that reflect the articulated needs of all persons involved.

The question of constituency is critical to any redistribution of power. One example of this dynamic is in the area of sexuality. A failure to challenge the dominant system's assumptions concerning sexuality and life-style functions to maintain prevailing patterns. In appointing committees to study human sexuality, theological institutions, church bodies, and women's groups select one lesbian and/or gay male to "speak" on behalf of *all* gay people, thus perpetuating tokenism and inequitable access to decision-making in the area of sexuality in the church. One result is that the frequent requirement by pastoral counselors that lesbians and gay men confess the "sinfulness" of their sexual preference in order to receive counseling remains unchallenged. An inequitable distribution of the church's resources is thus perpetuated. Such practices negate emerging models of "power with" and "empowerment," and maintain hierarchical models with token representation of less powerful groups.

5. *The personal is political and the political is personal.*

This particular assumption has been described as a truism of the women's movement. The authors of chapter 5 have provided helpful clarification of one aspect of the phrase; that is, the personal is political. Their comments emphasize the systemic nature of oppression and the social nature of issues that are most frequently described as personal. Our experiences within theological education have also shown us the personal implications of certain issues which have seemed primarily political in nature; for example, seminary budgets or fund-raising. The priorities established by the fund-raiser and the resources *he* seeks have a direct impact on the funding of educational and support services that are made available to women students and that affect personal experiences of women within theological institutions. The personal and political are integrally related, not dichotomously opposed to each other.

6. *As persons we have the right to control our own lives, including our bodies;* and

7. *As feminists we share a commitment to developing a worldview through a collective process that is inclusive of persons of differing race, class, sex, age, sexual preference, nationality, and faith.*

In describing the right to control our own lives, we are speaking of the right to real (not fictitious) choices and of the right to equal (not absolute) control in personal and social relations. We affirm our right to shape the context of our lives, while recognizing that we are also shaped through

111

interactions with other persons and within institutions. Such individual control may seem contradictory to our commitment to an inclusive worldview. Analyses of our experiences within theological education and of our alternative spaces have revealed some aspects of this conflict. To the extent that feminist and/or racial minority efforts in theological education accept the patriarchal structure of theology, politics, and economics, such conflicts will persist and exclusivity will be maintained. However, if the right to control our own lives is held in dynamic tension with the commitment to inclusivity, and power is equitably distributed in a nonhierarchical way, there is the possibility of developing pluralistic worldviews. It is only when we keep both these assumptions before us that we are able to affirm the struggle for liberation for all persons. When we shy away from developing pluralistic models and attempt to create one inclusive worldview, we show that we have misunderstood our own needs and have refused to establish bonds that would enable us to participate with others in their liberation struggles.

8. *Hope becomes present, manifesting itself in empowerment now rather than projected into a future vision.*
In the past ten years, during which women's programs have been taking root and transforming the soil of theological education, we have experienced both the excitement of creating alternative structures such as the Seminary Quarter at Grailville and the sobering recognition of failure to see and act against racism within our own alternatives. The process of constructive, self-critical reflection, then and now, on these experiences and of changes made within those structures to address acknowledged weaknesses has been an experience of hope-made-present. Hope-made-present happens because (a) we have asked questions that we have openly claimed as our own questions, not "universal" questions; (b) we have acted with

112

commitment with respect to those questions; (c) we have reflected on our initial questions and the consequences of our actions for ourselves and for others; (d) we have dared to risk reconceptualization of the questions, now more inclusive than before, leading us to new action. We affirm this process as hope-made-present, because we are continually empowered and energized by it.

As we experience an increased and shared sense of our empowerment, we find mainline institutions resisting changes more strongly. Such resistances lead not only to the need for increased efforts on our part, but also to the recognition that, in fact, we have made an impact on the dominant structure. When the dominant structures resist and seemingly lose control due to our presence, there is hope, because this increased resistance is an indication of the impact we are making and demonstrates that we have begun to transform their reality.

The creation of the programs described in this book and the reflective process that resulted in these pages are part of our journey as feminists in theological education. We have described our experiences, we have challenged and criticized one another, we have affirmed our successes, and we have learned from our failures. This journey is unlike most journeys described throughout Western literature. It is not the story of one hero who confronts the demon and emerges victorious. Rather, it is the journey of many women engaged in a collaborative struggle to confront sexism and racism in theological education. This book represents our description of that journey. It is an alternative in that we have unapologetically used our own experiences as a basis for developing our theological understanding. We have named these experiences and generalized from this base. We do not claim to have reached universal truth, but we have articulated assumptions that have applicability to all persons.

Further, our process presents an alternative in the

research methodology selected. As women in theological education, we are both the subject and the object of our study. As subjects, we have articulated questions that arise from our experiences. We have also been the objects of our critical reflections on these experiences, naming their strengths and their weaknesses. In becoming both the subjects and the objects of this research, we have transformed the dichotomy in terms of the ways in which questions have been raised and in terms of the applicability of our findings/learnings. These learnings lead directly to new questions and to the reconceptualization of the problems identified. It is to these learnings that we turn in summary.

First, our work describes the struggle of some women to confront racism and sexism in theological education. More specifically, it is a statement of how white women have confronted, with varying degrees of success, the racism of feminism and of mainline theological institutions. It is also a statement of how racial minority women, and in particular black women, have been willing to work with predominantly white women's organizations and to struggle to raise some of their questions within the context of the women's movement. That these black women and white women have chosen to work with each other and have struggled to learn how to collaborate is a statement that such cooperation is possible within theological education, if it is given high priority.

Second, the book represents a slight shift in power and in women's access to resources. By power we mean that women in theological education have chosen to speak out for themselves. We have collaborated with one another in sharing existing resources within the women's community, thus sustaining some of our alternative programs, such as SQAG. We have also confronted mainline institutions and have gained funding and support from the male establishment, or we have stepped outside that establishment, taking some of its resources with us, and have created our own programs. One such step is the writing of this book. Hence, it stands as a concrete statement of our access to power and to resources. Such a book could not have been written ten years ago. There were too few women in theological education and no women's programs. The women who were there were just beginning to be collectively aware of their marginalization and of the lack of educational opportunities and options available to them. It was partly through this experience of marginalization and the consequent struggles that we were able to create the programs described in these pages.

Third, working within these new programs has led us to new understandings of racism and of the class biases of theological education. Our concern with the context in which theological education occurs and our belief that the context informs and shapes the content must lead to the expansion of our constituencies beyond the school-educated elite. If not, the class bias and racism of theological education will not change. One way of responding to this particular learning is by being more attentive to the ways in which we define our issues and the programs we design to address them. The shift in SQAG from a national to a regional program, including the shift to a program that is more focused on specific issues and on skill development, is one such program. The experience of making this shift has been difficult for all, because we believed in the positive aspects of SQAG as it formerly existed. But we chose not to perpetuate its class bias and its racism. Our resistances to change provided us with insight into the response we have often felt from people in more established institutions who have been challenged to make significant changes within their structures. It also provided concrete exposure to the problems we face in mainline theological schools, as we struggle to address the exclusionary admissions policies, sexist hiring and promotion practices, and racist and sexist curricula.

We have further noted the impact of our work beyond the theological seminary or divinity school. Our programs have influenced and changed the perceptions, assumptions, and actions of numerous women now involved in ministry. Church structures, nonseminary women's centers, women's organizations, and professional church-women's associations have felt the effect of the work done on the issues described in this book. Across the nation we find denominational women's caucuses, legislative public hearings wherein "religious testimony" is often based on feminist theologizing, and seminars on "women doing theology" for local and regional groups occurring with greater frequency. Yet, there is a thundering silence in local churches and in ecumenical/interfaith councils even on such issues as inclusive, nonsexist language. We can attribute a portion of this silence to the problems women face in entering these structures and in achieving positions of leadership. In addition, we must recognize the lack of interest and overt resistances expressed by those who state that "these are not our issues" and "we've already dealt with that."

The gap between the vision we proclaim and the programs we have created is considerable. We have learned that to speak of nonsexist or nonracist education is not to create it. We have learned that our alternative structures and our women's programs within mainline institutions sometimes mirror the very institutions we are challenging and criticizing. Yet, through the reflective process we have more clearly discerned some of this mirroring and have begun the struggle to lessen the gap between feminist vision and reality. Hence, reflection forms an integral part of action in the ongoing struggle of women in theological education.

The scene has changed. When many of us entered seminaries and divinity schools there were few women students and fewer, if any, women faculty members or administrators. To enter that context was to enter an experience of marginality and alienation. The experience of marginality was partly responsible for consciousness-raising and the radicalization of many of us.

The context has shifted in several very concrete ways. There are more women in seminaries. One generally enters a situation where other women are seemingly comfortable. There are even a few women in positions of power. Many of the men use nonsexist language, and bibliographies include the writings of feminist theologians. These changes, seemingly for the better, also have a negative dimension: the experience of belonging, of being part of theological education, has minimized negative feelings of isolation but has also served to obfuscate the issue of sexism. Many white women do not think there is a problem for women in theological education. They do not experience exclusion from power or access to resources due to their sex. Hence, they are surprised when feminists describe racism in hiring and promotion or the sexism of the curriculum. Not having to confront the experience of tokenism or marginality, these women are not aware that theirs is the experience of a fortunate few. It is now the feminist who experiences further exclusion and marginality not merely from the mainline predominantly white male institution, but from other women. Hence, the task of those women committed to the elimination of racism and sexism within theological education and the church must also include raising the consciousness of other women. Unless our programs explicitly address racism and articulate the systemic nature of sexism, they may become part of the problem, serving to mask rather than eliminate the oppression of women. As creators of alternatives within the mainline institutions, we must guard against being co-opted and used to perpetuate the very system we have sought to change.

The task for feminists engaged in theological education and committed to working toward justice and liberation is complex. This record of our experiences represents only a small portion of a struggle that has continued for more than half a century. We share these experiences, hoping they will provide insights and clues for action that others may find useful. We have found the struggle itself energizing, and the telling of our story has been, for us, an effective tool for self-criticism and a vehicle for change.

Appendixes

The following appendixes provide summaries of the programs discussed in this book. The summaries have been adapted by Nancy Richardson from working papers prepared by program participants and used as the basic resource material for the book. For further information about the programs, contact the program offices directly.

The Center for Women and Religion of the Graduate Theological Union

History

The Center for Women and Religion (CWR) began as the Office of Woman's Affairs (OWA) *at* the Graduate Theological Union (GTU). Part of its history can be traced in the long debate about whether to change that preposition to "of," which was finally done nearly four years after the first cluster of women pooled their energies to bring OWA to birth, in 1970. From the start these women were conscious of the dangerous mission upon which women were about to embark in theological education and, beyond that, into the church, and they were wary about being "of" the same cloth as the structures from whence they perceived their oppression emanating. Wise women they were, and industrious and indomitable. The final arbiters of this debate in OWA were the need to stabilize funding, the recognition that work needed to be done within the structures on questions of the status of women, curriculum development, and other related issues that they could not do from the "outside." On the question of funding, GTU required OWA to become a sponsored group before it would even consider making a contribution to the budget.

Affiliation, however, did not end the marginalization in GTU seminaries, GTU structures, in the way theological education is conceived, the way decisions are made, nor in the content of the courses.

From the beginning, OWA/CWR had conceived of its work as having three foci: research; the status of women in the structures; and community-building for women students, faculty, staff, and spouses. It hoped to develop a women's studies research center and to foster the growth of women's consciousness, concerns, and caucuses to press for change on a wide range of issues. Affiliation did strengthen the funding needs of OWA/CWR to some degree. GTU actively pursued the proposal to the Ford Foundation, which culminated in a grant of $75,000 for a Visiting Scholars Program. The cost of that assistance was the normal 23%, which remained with GTU for administrative costs, leaving $57,000 for the three-year program.

The struggle to be heard in the GTU context has produced a rich mix of significant programs, publications, events, courses, and a large number of women whose lives attest to the power and strength CWR has helped to bring into focus for them. Two books have been published with the assistance of the office: *Women and the Word, Toward a Whole Theology* and *Women in a Strange Land.* A packet of resources for women's consciousness-raising in churches is still being sold nationally, and a bibliography is widely used and still selling well (it is currently being revised). We have sponsored several outstanding conferences (Racism/Sexism and Lesbianism/Feminism) and numerous one-day events.

Structure

The structure of CWR is that of a center with several program aspects. It has a multiple staff, currently made up of two part-time coordinators/directors and four work/

study students. A policy-making steering committee is composed of fifteen members. It does its work through two major task forces: personnel, and planning and development. Other task forces form as needed and are designated by the mysterious-sounding terminology of "disappearing task force," meaning that they self-destruct when their tasks are over. CWR serves a multiple constituency of women in the seminaries of GTU and the GTU graduate programs, spouses, and women faculty. In an informal way, it serves as a resource and information center for a wider Bay Area constituency of church women.

Sources of Funding

It is funded principally through grants from eight of the nine seminaries, and from GTU. About 80% of our funds come from this source. The remainder of our income comes from donations, gifts, and small grants from various foundations.

Assumptions Behind the Program Design

CWR now, and OWA before it, worked on the assumption that the transformation of theological education toward wholeness is essential and is possible. It is a political process, and we have to proceed from that difficult reality: change does not happen—we make it happen. We are therefore engaged in the effort to describe the human more fully. In this setting it requires faculty who are capable of the arduous task of looking at their material afresh, faculty who embody in themselves the wholeness that has been distorted, and administrators who are willing to look beyond the expedient in their commitments to women seminarians and to theological excellence in general. The commitment to curriculum development proceeds from these assumptions.

We are also engaged in the development of a women's community that can voice its own needs to the seminaries, that can be empowered to work for institutional change by being involved in action while in seminary, and that can find its own way of ministering to other women in the GTU setting.

The issues that are currently being addressed are the fundamental patriarchal mentality that pervades Judeo-Christian theology, and the culture, values, mores, institutions that have developed from that matrix; the questions of power/powerlessness that women have experienced both in the church and in society and culture, and that are reflected in the organizational life of CWR vis-à-vis GTU and the seminaries. A specific and long-term concern has been with the issue of sexuality as a fundamental question of personal autonomy and social justice.

Relationships to the GTU

We are a sponsored center of the GTU. We participate in the Consortium Council, a body that recommends programs and policies for the collective member schools; and we participate on an ad hoc basis in the agendae of other consortium entities (GTU Board of Trustees, Heads Meetings) and in the agendae of faculty, curriculum, and trustee meetings at member schools. In addition, at San Francisco Theological School we have a formal annual contract for funds received and services rendered.

Primary Questions/Most Urgent Problems

The question of autonomy as it relates to funding. . . . The question of credibility and visibility in a bureaucratic structure when we are working on new approaches to organization, structure, and staffing models.

123

—Adapted from a working
paper prepared by Peggy
Cleveland and Barbara
Waugh

For more information contact:
Center for Women and Reli-
gion
Graduate Theological Union
2465 LeConte Avenue
Berkeley, CA 94709

The Women's Theological Coalition Boston Theological Institute

History

The beginning of the Women's Theological Coalition (WTC) can be traced to 1970—to the report of the National Conference on the Role of Women in Theological Education, which became the founding document of a "Women's Institute" in the Boston Theological Institute (BTI). The focus of the Women's Institute was primarily academic: the goals of the institute were more women students, more women's studies courses, and more women faculty.

The style and tactics of the women involved in the institute were frequently confrontational. Partly this was a reflection of the objectively difficult situation in which the women found themselves. A tiny minority of the whole BTI, they had to fight hard for recognition and funding with the school deans (who form the executive committee), who were attempting to allocate BTI's limited resources among a number of competing interests.

In 1973, there were major changes, with a shift in emphasis from academic to ministry issues. The institute changed its name to the Women's Theological Coalition and increasingly stressed cooperation, mutual under-standing, and inclusiveness of diverse feminist prspectives. The change had a salutary effect on the BTI governing structure: in the middle of the 1973-74 academic year the trustees of BTI voted to guarantee WTC a $17,500 annual budget for a period of three years. Yet, it is clear that the present WTC would not be as firmly "established" as it is had it not been for the sometimes "extreme" actions of the first leaders of the Women's Institute.

Also in 1973-74 WTC secured its first grant from outside sources. The Ford Foundation made a $15,000 grant to support the Doctoral Placement Service for Women in Religious Studies as a national service; the next year the Rockefeller Family Fund made a grant for the Placement of Women in Parish Ministries project.

Structure

A Women's Committee—composed of two students repre-senting each BTI member school, two faculty representa-tives, and several community-at-large representatives—is the planning and decision-making body for the WTC.

WTC has a staff, paid from the BTI/WTC budget, that meets regularly to make administrative decisions on a collective basis. The staff consists of a coordinator; a student chairperson of the Women's Committee; an office manager; the editor of the WTC monthly newsletter, *Affirmations*; and a resources coordinator. In addition, foundation grants pay the salaries of the administrator of the Doctoral Placement Service and a consultant for the Placement of Women in Parish Ministries project. (All staff, except the coordinator and the placement consultant, are BTI students; all staff, including the coordinator, are part-time. The coordinator is half-time; the students work ten to twenty hours a week.)

The WTC is represented on the formal councils of the BTI. The coordinator and the chairperson attend the monthly meetings of the BTI executive committee and the semiannual meetings of the board of trustees with voice but not vote. In official parlance, the WTC is a standing committee of the BTI.

Constituency

The WTC's constituency is difficult to define. The primary constituency is clearly the women students and the women faculty of BTI. But there is a constituency, or potential constituency, beyond students and faculty. Some student spouses participate in WTC programs. There is an effort to meet the needs of the women staff. In addition, at least one program event each year is designed to include women in both lay and ordained ministries in the metropolitan area.

Programs and Assumptions

The programs of the WTC are multifaceted, reflecting what is the primary assumption, or operating principle, of the coalition in its present form—its diversity and inclusiveness.

The diversity can be seen in the programs that the Women's Committee itself plans and implements; these range from lectures on topics that interest primarily women ministers/theology students to workshops produced primarily for laywomen. This diversity can also be seen in the programs the WTC cosponsors with others each year, including various activities (conferences, lectures, workshops, research projects) produced for and by evangelical women, Roman Catholic women, lesbians in ministry—the spread is vast, as are the program topics.

127

Primary Questions and Urgent Problems

How do we do advocacy—deciding whom we represent and dealing with the ways our institutional affiliation is affected by our advocacy stance? . . . How to work with entering women students who are frequently unaware of the battles fought by a generation of women who were adamant for change and politically aware. . . . Balancing local (BTI) and national program interests—dealing with overcommitment, limited staff and financial resources. . . . How to work most supportively with black and other racial minority women. . . . Dealing with our own racism (and class biases)—these are perhaps the most serious problems we face.

> —Adapted from a working paper prepared by Barbara Wheeler

> For more information contact: Women's Theological Coalition
> 210 Herrick Road
> Newton Centre, MA 02159

128

Black Women in Ministry Boston Theological Institute

History and Assumptions

The history of black women in the ministry is contiguous with the historical struggle of black people for liberation from oppression. Black Women in Ministry (BWIM) began as a response from black women who believed and tried to live the gospel message, and who felt called to ministry.

The goal of this project was to provide opportunities for black women to develop effective, diverse ministries; to develop support systems for black women; and to advocate for the role of black women in church leadership and other professional ministry. BWIM seeks to address the needs of black women—lay and ordained—who are engaged in diverse ministries.

There are only about twenty black women currently enrolled in all BTI-member schools. BWIM functions as a means of support to those black women who are, amid the struggle, giving strength and nurturance to the few women we have. BWIM seeks to address the needs of black women in a society that too often sees us as nonpeople. It creates a space for black women defined by the very participants.

Assumptions and Issues

BWIM strives to develop contexts for the practice of

ministry in which the significant contribution of black women is recognized. In addition to sponsoring and participating in both regional and national conferences, the organization develops workshops, publicizes local resources, and works closely with related church and seminary groups. Affirming the richness of the black church—in the various forms in which it is expressed—and its position in the church universal, BWIM joins efforts with all peoples and groups, regardless of their ethnic background or sex, who seriously heed the gospel's mandate of liberation.

Problems

The problems we in BWIM face now are very much the same ones that called us into existence. First, we are a group of overextended individuals who do not need one more commitment added to our resonsibilities. Whether because of the pressures from family life, or economic need, or the hectic schedule of being token members on both denominational and ecumenical boards, or the psychic drain of living/studying/working in a world that does not recognize our existence, we are often tired and must conscientiously set priorities in our lives. Also, many black women form a critical—if not suspicious—audience. We do not have the energies to continually plunge into the unknown or to be a joiner. Last, our greatest asset—diversity—poses organizational difficulties. Within BWIM are represented old and young; ordained, seminarian, and lay; Pentecostal and Catholic; predominantly white denominations and traditionally black churches; those calling themselves feminists and others not choosing that designation. To develop programming that addresses the various needs and perspectives is no mean task.

Future Directions

Where do we go from here? Hopefully there will come a time when our existence will no longer be needed: when there will be a substantial body of black women seminarians to offer mutual support and develop advocacy; when denominations, pulpits, chaplaincies, and social outreach programs will be open to black women ministers and lay leaders; when the diversity of religious experiences and gifts will be recognized. Such is not likely to occur tomorrow or the day after. Until then, black Christian women need to come together, affirming our heritage, developing our talents, and creating paths for others to follow.

—Adapted from a working paper prepared by Adele Smith-Penniman and Cheryl Giles

For more information contact:
Black Women in Ministry
45 Francis Avenue
Cambridge, MA 02138

Research/Resource Associates Program Harvard Divinity School

History, Structure, and Assumptions

Five women joined the Harvard Divinity School as Research/Resource Associates in women's studies in the fall of 1973. Five associates have been appointed to the program in each succeeding year. The program seeks, through research, to articulate perspectives relating to the role, status, image, and ethical concerns of women in the various religious traditions, and to address the needs for curriculum development resulting from a feminist analysis of theological education. The responsibilities of the associates include (1) research (a project on a specific question relating to women), (2) resource (development of library resources, additions to course bibliography, film, music, and art resources), (3) curriculum evaluation and development. The original proposal recommended that there be at least five associates and that the group be interracial, to reflect the concerns of all women. From its inception the program has sought to address the needs and reflect the reality of racial minority women as well as white women.

During its first year the program was coordinated by one of the associates. Since the fall of 1974 it has been administered and coordinated by the coordinator of

Women's Programs. Total funding for the program has been provided by Harvard Divinity School. By creating research/resource associates who were neither faculty nor students, it was hoped to introduce a new way of being in the academy. The appointment of five associates sought to reinforce a commitment to collegial and interdisciplinary studies, and to provide a model that would maintain a tension between theory and praxis.

Strategies

The strategies for developing and implementing the program were a combination of grass-roots constituency-based organizing and consciousness-raising among male students and faculty, followed by work through the established procedures of the school for introducing new programming. In the fall of 1973 the Committee on Women's Programs was established as a standing commit-tee of the faculty. It is composed of students and faculty, and is charged with overseeing existing programs and recommending new programs to the faculty.

Primary Questions/Most Urgent Problems

The program is directly related to the school through the office of the coordinator of Women's Programs. Much discussion of the program has focused on the nature of the changes implemented by the program. Little has been accomplished in the area of substantive curricular change or in terms of systemic change at Harvard Divinity School. However, notable changes have occurred in personal growth, political and spiritual consciousness-raising, and in the discovery of new areas of research and new method-ologies within the theological disciplines.

Because the research/resource associates are part-time,

short-term, and low in pay and in status, they have minimal impact on the system; at the same time, they allow Harvard to claim it has a women's studies program without requiring the school to hire full-time women on the faculty. This program does not negate the importance of hiring women full-time on the faculty. The associates provide resources and services in areas that must be addressed, and they have provided a context for the development of women scholars and educators in religion, while also providing organizers within the school.

Major Themes

The major issues with which the program continues to struggle include struggle for survival (both in terms of faculty support and in terms of funding); ability to address the needs of all women—black, Hispanic, Asian, and white; creation of an alternative space for women within the institution; the ongoing struggle to change the system.

The Future

Several suggestions include the possibility of more collective work among the associates, including studying one area or problem from an interdisciplinary perspective or teaching an introductory course on feminist studies in theological education.

The historical situation has changed in seminaries: no longer are women a numerical minority; the women's movement has crested as a movement. Many men who briefly tolerated the movement have retrenched and become rigid opponents. Sexism has become more subtle in some instances but has not abated. Many women students in seminaries were not involved in the struggles for present gains and do not identify with the women's movement. In some ways the Research/Resource Associates must be engaged in consciousness-raising among the students as well as with the faculty. Both the mood of the university-based seminary and that of women are changing. Any examination and evaluation of the program must examine it in relationship to these changes and make recommendations for the future.

—Adapted from a working paper prepared by Brinton Lykes

For more information contact:
Office of Women's Programs
Harvard Divinity School
45 Francis Avenue
Cambridge, MA 02138

Seminary Quarter at Grailville

History

Seminary Quarter at Grailville (SQAG) grew out of two week-long seminars—"Women Exploring Theology"—held at Grailville, Loveland, Ohio, in the summer of 1972 and of 1973. The seminary women who had been part of these experiences asked for a similar program focused directly on their concerns. A planning group including representatives from United Methodist Women, United Theological Seminary, Methodist Commission on the Status of Women, National Council of Churches, and Grailville was formed. This group contacted resource people, hired a coordinator, located staff, looked for funding, and inaugurated the first Seminary Quarter in June 1974.

Seminary Quarter is unique in that it is a substantial unit of theological education (a summer quarter, offering two units or eight quarter-hours of bona fide credit) in which women's concerns are central rather than peripheral. Important elements in the model include:

—women theologians as role models
—the building of a living/learning community in which everyone shares in the decision-making by which the group constitutes itself

—a self-directed learning model in which individuals and groups focus their own questions and methods of study

—a wholistic and experimental approach to learning, uniting intellect and emotion, using all modes of perception and expression

—a focus on feminist perspectives, both in critiquing traditional studies and in breaking new ground by theological reflection on women's experience.

Structure

The basic structure, responsible for overall direction and decision-making, is the advisory committee. Its twenty members meet twice a year and work through four subgroups for personnel, finance, interpretation (which includes evaluation and public relations), and NPP (networking, planning, and projection). Each SQAG group elects a representative, as does each SQAG staff, the Grailville staff, and the Commission on Women in Ministry (COWIM). Otherwise, the committee is self-perpetuating. In the fall of 1976 we moved to one salaried year-round administrator on a half-time basis.

Constituency

In the four years—1974 to 1977—eighty-four women from thirty-three schools (twenty-eight seminaries, five universities) have participated in SQAG. All the major denominations have been represented, from United Methodist to Unitarian, Roman Catholic to African Methodist Episcopal Zion, with the greatest number being United Methodist, United Church of Christ, or Presbyterian. Six racial minority women have taken part—five black, one Hispanic—and there have been three black staff members. No doubt the great majority would characterize themselves as middle class, but there have been a few upper-middle and working-class women as well.

Funding

There have been five major sources of funding: (1) student fees, which bring in about one third the budget through the students, own fund-raising efforts; (2) church agencies; (3) the Lilly Endowment; (4) individual donors; and (5) contributed services by volunteers.

Assumptions

The basic components of the program are listed above. Here are some of the basic assumptions underlying the choice of these components:

—That a short, intensive experience is of prime importance educationally and offers different opportunities for learning and growth than the conventional fragmented, departmentalized style of most academic programs.
—That it is crucial to integrate the cognitive and affective.
—That it is crucial to integrate theory and practice, action and reflection.
—That it is crucial to integrate the concrete and abstract, and therefore to use all means of perception and expression (body movement, music, the visual arts, direct experience of nature and materials).
—That human beings are naturally active, curious, and eager to learn; that therefore the primary task of the educator is to provide a rich learning environment.

—That a self-directed learning model is of particular importance for women, since it builds self-confidence in the learner.

—That in a self-directed model, peers are seen as resources, and resource persons are seen as co-learners.

—That to develop learning skills it is important to work both individually and in a collaborative group.

—That sexism cannot be understood apart from race and class and vice versa.

—That ultimately the personal is political; that personal growth, if it is authentic, will lead to social action; that social action which is not rooted in deep personal commitment will soon wither.

—That women, as part of the excluded majority, have vitalizing insights and creative energies to bring to theology and ministry at this time.

Institutional Relations

With respect to the seminaries, SQAG is totally outside the system, making an intervention with a strong ecumenical and interfaith thrust. It is linked to the Association of Theological Schools' credit system through United Theological Seminary in Dayton. SQAG had grown out of the matrix provided by COWIM and Grailville.

Strategies

The basic educational strategy is one of "the medium is the message"; that is, the endeavor to embody in the living/learning community a model of an alternative learning environment, incorporating certain ideal elements as fully as possible. The model is, at the same time, an experience of empowerment, an opportunity to deal with a new and unstructured situation, and preparation for taking initiative in bringing about social change.

Problems

A primary problem with which we are struggling at present is how to design the program so that both racial minority and working-class women can participate in much larger numbers, not only in the programs but in the planning. We are experimenting with regionalizing and urbanizing in the hope of moving toward a solution.

A second problem has to do with the tension between the emphasis on self-directed learning and our concern with some specific content.

Funding remains a perennial problem. There are also the problems related to institutional impact.

Themes/Issues

The major themes can be identified, in the broadest terms, as follows: language, myth, and symbol; sexuality; theology; and social change.

Projections for the Future

Important steps for the future:

—to continue network-building as a concrete manifestation of sisterhood; trying to identify that minority who name themselves both feminists and believers, that we may avoid duplication of effort and give one another support on the personal level and in our varied projects

—to regionalize, both in terms of SQAG as a program and in terms of follow-up to this consultation

—to create an environment in which black women and white women can theologize together.

—Adapted from a working paper prepared by Janet Kalven

For more information contact:
Women United in Theologizing and Action
Grailville
Loveland, OH 45140

Training Women for Ministry Andover Newton Theological School

History and Assumptions

Responding to questions raised by seminaries and denominational staffs about how to prepare women for ministry and help them find jobs, the United Church of Christ Task Force on Women and Society, at its meeting in the fall of 1973, chose the seminaries as a major focus for its work during the 1973-75 biennium.

A working group was assigned the task of exploring the needs of women in theological education and of making recommendations that would help the UCC in developing new educational models to prepare women for effective ministries in the church. The assumption was that a self-directed learning experience would help women in the defining and doing of ministry and would set a style of continuing education. The program was intended to demonstrate methods that could then be used by other seminaries. The task force selected the Department of Church and Ministry at Andover Newton Theological School as the site for developing and testing this experimental program.

Participants

A *steering committee* was established to advise the ministry team and oversee evaluation of the program.

A *ministry team* to teach the course was selected on the basis of the following criteria: experience in ministry, theological training, grasp of educational goals of the program, ability to work in a team, personal style as a viable model for ministry, representatives of a variety of ministries. The first two years all three team members were white. At the end of the second year of the program the need for racial diversity was identified as a major concern. An intentional search process surfaced a wealth of experienced applicants, and a black woman was hired.

Students were drawn from the nine schools of the Boston Theological Institute. Except for one Hispanic woman, from Puerto Rico, students have been exclusively white.

Design

The educational method was based upon the assumption that students were capable of directing their own learning.

Through the first three experimental years the academic year's work culminated in individual summer projects, where students worked full-time in ministry that reflected their own vocational goals. When the course was incorporated as a regular part of the seminary curriculum, this summer component was absorbed as a field education project.

Some Key Factors

As the program has developed over the years it has been possible to identify some of the elements necessary for the program to meet its goals. Some of these elements proved

143

to be strengths. Others have been identified as areas that need improvement.

1. Commitment: the high degree of personal commitment to and responsibility for both group and individual work was perhaps the most important variable in the program.
2. Diversity: the diversity among the students—in their traditions, personalities, circumstances, goals, and talents—emerged as one of the real strengths of the program.
3. Process: attention to the process was both a necessity and a strength. Especially important were shared leadership and shared responsibility.
4. Team approach: multiple leadership had several good effects; to the extent that it was successful, the ministry team set a pattern for leadership and exposed students to a variety of models for women in ministry. But working as a team was not always easy or successful. Collective planning and evaluation continue to be experimental. Differences within the leadership were often glossed over, and conflicts were avoided rather than used to advantage in planning and facilitating the course.

An Assessment

After three years of the program's operation it is possible to say that it is working to ameliorate several problems that have plagued women working in and aspiring to ministry: isolation, visibility, vocational identity, and power. It has provided an effective model for seminary education—in the use of a team approach and in the involvement of practicing ministries in the education experience.

As an experimental program especially geared toward the education of women seminarians, the program demonstrated a financially feasible way to ensure the presence of women teacher-ministers on campus as role models and resource persons. However, basic and persistent educational questions remain that do not invite easy solutions; the questions now concern internal vs. external motivation and issues of faith and theology.

Projections for the Future

At this point it looks like the self-directed learning model will be adopted by the seminary. Andover Newton has committed itself to assuming the cost of the program, which has now been adapted to reduce costs. One of the big questions is how long such a program aimed only at women in ministry will be necessary. Such a model of self-directed learning and the utilization of practicing ministers in the training of students for ministry is definitely an educational method that would be beneficial to all students.

> —Adapted from a working paper compiled by Catherine Chiffelle and Barbara Gerlach, who updated and abridged an article by Barbara Gerlach and Emily Hewitt, "Training Women for Ministry," published in the *Andover Newton Quarterly,* vol. 17, no. 2 (November 1976).
>
> For more information contact:
> Andover Newton Theological School
> Department of Church and Ministry
> 210 Herrick Road
> Newton Centre, MA 02159

Women Counseling Team Union Theological Seminary

The team is one of three bodies at the seminary which are responsive to women's issues and needs. The Women Counseling Team (WCT) is actually the least "woman-specific" of the three.

The Program

The WCT is a group of four women who function as a team to do counseling, advisement, research, and programming around women's issues and needs, particularly as the latter relate specifically to women in ministry and theological education.

History

The WCT was born in the spring of 1973 as a result of suggestions emerging from a Consultation on Women at Union that women students need help connecting and integrating their field work experience, coursework, and vocational aspirations. The larger context that encompasses the consultation is the resolution made by the board of directors, in 1972, to work toward achieving a student ratio of half women and one third blacks, and approximately the same ratio for the faculty. This goal with regard to women has been reached in the student body but remains very distant with regard to the faculty, leaving a great need for more women at the seminary as role models for teaching and parish ministry, and for advisement and counseling. The formation of the WCT was, in large part, an attempt to remedy this in a temporary fashion and also to respond to the above-mentioned needs.

Structure

There are four positions on the team, each of which is a loosely designated area of competence: the coordinator, the academic advisor, the administrative assistant in the dean of students' office, and a programming assistant to the dean of students' office. The coordinator and the academic advisor meet regularly with the dean of students and the academic dean respectively, who act as supervisors. The general structure is nonhierarchical and involves a combination of team and individual work in the designated but overlapping areas of competence and interest.

Whom We Serve

The WCT is primarily devoted to helping women students, but there are, of course, many aspects of "women's issues" that benefit men. Its services are available to all who choose to make use of them.

Funding

Our budget consists of two salaries and a small expense account, funded through the academic office of the seminary. Two of the team members, the administrative assistant in the dean of students' office and the programming assistant, are employed directly through the dean of students' office and, rather than receive additional pay as members of the WCT, they are allowed time from their primary positions to participate on the team.

Assumptions

The design of the program assumes that, because of the relative exclusion of women and the long-standing insensitivity to their desire to participate fully in Christian ministry, women seminarians and graduate students of theology face problems and have needs particular to their situation. The WCT's components correspond to its purpose, which is to provide a wholistic approach to field, vocational, and academic advisement.

Primary Questions/Problems

Our most general question/problem involves how we can address the concerns of the greatest number in the very diverse student body at Union. Basically, our problems are (1) being low on the seminary's list of priorities and (2) the fact that issues surrounding women in ministry are not ultimately seen as serious matters for the entire seminary. Women's issues remain peripheral, and efforts to fulfill the commitment to women in seminary education continue to take the form of specialty courses and tokenism.

Major Themes/Issues

The themes and issues that are part of the WCT's work include:

—finding and evaluating opportunities for, experiences of, women in fieldwork situations.

148

—the problem of inadequate numbers of women to serve as role models.

—the need for advocacy around women's issues.

—the need to develop new models for ministry.

—student assessment of courses.

—the extent to which women's concerns are excluded from the basic curriculum on the pretext of the need for "objective scholarship": the need to integrate them.

—spirituality/worship/community.

—sexuality, relationship, life-style.

—student/faculty communication.

—racism, heterosexism; the problems and concerns of black students and gay students; responding to the situation of black women whose situation at the seminary is especially bleak.

Projections for the Future

The vision is one of integration. We hope for our eventual obsolescence, which will coincide with acquiring adequate numbers of women on the faculty and the administration to serve the needs of seminary women. It will coincide with the seminary's acknowledgment of the problem of sexism (not separate from heterosexism) as a serious one, requiring significant changes in the curriculum and in academic policies.

—Adapted from a working paper prepared by Susan Moyes

For more information contact:
Women Counseling Team
Union Theological Seminary
120th St. at Broadway
New York, NY 10027

Notes

Introduction

1. Unless otherwise noted (as in chapters 3 and 4), "we" and "our" in this book refer to the authors, i.e., to the women who helped write the book by writing working papers, by participating in the consultation described below, or by contributing to chapters in the final manuscript.

2. This definition of sexism is based on a definition of racism developed by Robert Terry and used in a conference, "New White Consciousness," at Colombiere College, north of Detroit, Michigan, in 1971. See chapter 3 for a more detailed discussion of our understanding of the relationship between racism and sexism, and how this definition helps us in that understanding.

3. Members of the coordinating committee were Janet Kalven, Brinton Lykes, Joan Martin, Lynn Rhodes, and Nancy Richardson (chairperson), all of whom were also consultation participants (see pages xvii-xix for a complete list of participants).

4. The consultation was funded by the Lilly Endowment as a part of its grant to Seminary Quarter at Grailville.

5. Summaries of the working papers are included in the appendixes.

Chapter 1 Toward a Feminist Understanding of Theological Education

1. "Why the Seminary," an introduction to the report of the Auburn History Project, a study funded by the Lilly Endowment, to be published in 1981, p. 13.

2. Ibid., p. 56.

3. Paulo Freire, *Pedagogy of the Oppressed* (New York: Seabury Press, 1970), chapter 2.

4. The term "racial minority" is used here and throughout this

150

book, to refer to persons of African, Asian, Hispanic, and indigenous Indian descent, since we are dealing with a North American, and more particularly, a United States context. In a global context the term would, of course, more accurately refer to persons of Caucasian descent.

5. Since the Cornwall Consultation, the R/RA Program has undergone a major evaluation, and substantial changes in the program have been proposed for 1980 and 1981. It is yet to be determined how these changes will affect the curriculum.

6. "The Lady Who Used to Be a Strawberry," unpublished anthology, edited by Elaine C. Huber, compiled by Jeannie Gross (Berkeley, CA: Center for Women and Religion).

7. One woman in the class wrote:

god damn. i haven't through my tradition come out with
sacred places, relics, times—
but my insides find so many things sacred—so many times—
space-time wholeness/holiness experience
places i have melded with—
    rocks and spaces my body curves with just as
    it curves with another body.

—Dixie Jennings

Ibid., p. 15. Used by permission of the Center for Women and Religion.

Another woman wrote:

I do not know
whether the world
plays the part
of the ultimate
oppressor
and I the victim
or
whether
in my
inability to face
the world

151

I
must by
force
become its ultimate
oppressor.

—Kathleen Kent

Ibid., p. 24. Used by permission of the author.

8. In the fall of 1979 the Training Women for Ministry program was incorporated into the regular curriculum of Andover Newton Theological School; it will be offered on alternate years.

Chapter 2 Constituency: What We Learn Is Shaped by Those with Whom We Learn

1.William Ryan, *Blaming the Victim* (New York: Vintage Books, 1976 [revised edition]), p. 137.

Chapter 3 Racism and the Responsibilities of White Women in Theological Education

1. Robert Terry has developed a graphic representation of this phenomenon.

	Active	Passive
Racist	Bigotry Discrimination	Status Quo
Antiracist	Change	X

The box shown here is divided horizontally to represent racist and antiracist behavior, and vertically to represent active and passive approaches to racism. As indicated, an active racist is one who is a bigot or who uses the power of racism to actively, intentionally discriminate against persons on the basis of color. The passive racist is one who does nothing about racism and thereby allows the status quo (which *is* racist) to continue as it is. The active antiracist is one who takes responsibility for his/her own racism and actively works for personal and institutional change. Most liberals would like to be passive antiracist—i.e., give lip service to the elimination of racism but do nothing else. But this is impossible, because to be passive is to maintain the status quo and thus to perpetuate racism. This was presented by Robert Terry in a conference, "New White Consciousness: Prerequisite for Change in America," sponsored by Detroit Industrial Mission and New Detroit, Inc. Speakers Bureau, May 19-23, 1971, Colombiere College, north of Detroit, Michigan.

2. See Robert W. Terry, *For Whites Only* (Grand Rapids, Mich.: Wm. B. Eerdmans, 1970) for a more detailed analysis of the differences between these concepts.

3. The use of "we" and "our" is problematic in this chapter. The reflection on the issue of racism took place in a group consisting of one black woman and four white women. Learnings from those reflections thus grow out of a dialogue in which the "we" and "our" are black women and white women. Since it is clear that what we learn is shaped by how and with whom to learn, the "we" that constitutes the reflection groups is particularly significant on this subject. At other points in the paper, reference is made to white racism. Here "we" and "our" refer to white women and the work that must be done among white women if the issue of racism is to be dealt with seriously.

4. It is important to note that while the definitions of sexism and racism used in this book have some important similarities, we do not understand them to be identical. Their similarities grow out of an understanding of power. Those who have power are able to determine the distribution of resources, to make and enforce decisions, to set standards for appropriate behavior, and to define reality—all of which are components of the definition of racism developed by Robert Terry (see note 2 in the Introduction) and used in this book in reference to sexism as well as racism. The differences between racism and sexism have to do with different historical realities and different degrees of accessibility to power between white women and racial minority persons. Some examples of this difference include:

a. The relationship of white women to those in power (i.e., white men) is radically different from the relationship of people of color to those in power (i.e., white women are their daughters, mothers, sisters, wives).

b. The reality of slavery has been a historical determinant in the "legitimization" of the cultural, political, economic exclusion of people of color from power.

c. Racism has created the myth that white people are the majority in the world and therefore have a right to control the world. White people are, in fact, in power in the world. White women participate in that power and therefore in the racism that created and maintains the myth.

Chapter 4 Marginality, Alternative Structures, and Leadership Styles

1. Here again note must be taken of some historical and sociological differences between black women and white women. White women in this culture have been socialized to believe that their needs will be met, perhaps even more readily, if they remain powerless, and thus they have learned not to think of themselves as powerful, not to want power, even to consider themselves as above wanting to have or use power. Black women, however, have been excluded not only from systemic power, but from access to the powerful (white males) which white women have had. As a result, black women tend to understand the importance of power and to be more positively inclined toward its use than white women. See chapter 5 for a more detailed discussion of this.

2. Judith Bardwick, "Some Notes About Power Relationships Between Women" in *Beyond Sex Roles*, ed. Alice Sargent (St. Paul, Minn.: West Publishing, 1977), p. 331. Reprinted by permission of West Publishing Company. Copyright © 1977. All rights reserved.

3. In this section "we" and "our" refer not only to the authors, but to our understanding of the experience of women in the larger society.

Chapter 5 Power and Institutional Change

1. An excellent discussion of the issue of sexual harassment and strategies for dealing with it is found in *Frying Pan*, June 1978, pp. 28-29.

2. Charlotte Bunch, "The Reform Tool Kit," *Quest*, vol. I, no. 1 (Summer 1974), pp. 39ff.

3. Marilyn Frye, "Who Wants a Piece of the Pie," *Quest*, vol. III, no. 3 (Winter 1976-77), pp. 31-32. Used by permission.

4. Amelie Ratliff, "Beverly Harrison: Living with Contradiction," *Walking Together*, 1977 Seminary Quarter at Grailville booklet, Loveland, Ohio, p. 58. Based on a lecture given by Dr. Harrison for participants in the 1977 Seminary Quarter at Grailville. Used by permission.

5. Ibid.

Index

abortion, 44, 99
academic discipline, 2-3, 9
access, 78-79, 106-7
accountability, 82
advocacy role, 52, 89, 98
aggression, 60-61
Alinsky, Saul, 91
alternative services, 85
alternative spaces, 54-58, 75, 85-86
alternative structures, xx, 11, 74-75, 84-85, 116
Andover curriculum, 3
Andover Newton Theological School, 71, 89
Andover Newton Theological School Women's Resource Center, 30
Andover Theological Seminary, 2
antiwar movement, viii
assertiveness, 79-80
Association of Theological Schools, 49-50

Bardwick, Judith, 60
Bennett, Anne, viii
blacks, 5, 36, 49, 55
  importance of family, 21, 31
black women, 8, 15, 20, 23, 31, 40, 44-45, 48, 56, 82-83, 107-8
  and Black Power movement, 20

as leaders in church, 8, 22-24, 48, 56, 83-84, 114
relationship with black church, 21-23, 84
survival as issue, 21, 56, 83
and white institutions, 20-24, 56
Black Women and Black Religious Experience, 8
Black Women in Ministry (BWIM), xiv, 8, 10, 12, 15, 36, 55, 98
boards as decision-makers, 52, 66, 73
  working boards, 71-73
Boston Theological Institute (BTI), 30, 38, 56, 71-72, 89, 94, 98-100
Brigham Young University, 90
budgets
  and decision-making, 72
  as means of control, 33
Bunch, Charlotte, 102-3

caste, 27
caste system, 65-66
Catholic, 24, 36
Catholic Women's Ordination Conference, 91-92
celibacy, 28
Center for Women and Religion (CWR), xiv, 7, 10, 12, 47, 57, 64, 71-73, 86, 91, 98-101
Christianity, 28-29, 35, 79

157

159

victim role, 60-61
Visiting Scholar Program, 57

wealth, 27
Weber, Max, 27
white male perspective, 4, 12-16,
    28, 35, 44-45
wholistic, 67
wholistic education, xiv, 7-8, 31,
    57
women
    administrators, 50-51
    black, 8, 15, 20, 31, 40, 44-45
    in Christian thought, 28-29
    and the church, ix, 17
    and class, 24
    faculty, 50, 100
    Hispanic, 15, 31
    Latin American, 15, 21
    lesbian, 15, 30-31
    male definition of, 16-17, 28-
        29, 32
    and ministry, 29, 100
    as nurturer, 17, 28-29, 65-66,
        79
    as oppressed, 4, 14-15, 17, 26,
        28-29, 43-44, 46
    as oppressors, 17, 22, 26, 43-
        44, 46

paternal role, 65-66
racial minority, 20-23, 31, 40,
    44, 48
racism in, 19-22, 42-44, 102
in seminary, 49-58, 117
single, 30
socialization of, 65-66, 79, 95
and theological education, vii,
    xiii, xv, xix, xxi, 5, 22, 57,
    78, 116
white, 20-22, 38, 40-48, 78-79,
    81, 83, 95
Women Counseling Team
    (WCT), xv, 19, 36, 39, 45,
    47, 89, 98,
women-identified women, 29, 32
Women's Caucus of the Ameri-
    can Academy of Religion,
    viii
Women's Equity Action League
    (WEAL), 89
women's movement, xiv, 10, 14-
    15, 58, 65, 85-86, 103
women's studies courses, 50-51,
    53, 59, 86, 100, 102
Women's Theological Coalition
    (WTC), xv, 30, 36, 38, 44,
    46, 48, 71-72, 94, 98-99
World Council of Churches, viii